CONSCIOUS MARKETING

How to create an awesome business with a new approach to marketing

CAROLYN TATE

WILEY

First published in 2015 by John Wiley & Sons Australia, Ltd
42 McDougall St, Milton Qld 4064

Office also in Melbourne

Typeset in 9.5/13.5 pt Goudy Oldstyle Std

© Carolyn Tate and Co. 2015

The moral rights of the author have been asserted

National Library of Australia Cataloguing-in-Publication data:

Creator:	Tate, Carolyn, author.
Title:	Conscious Marketing: how to create an awesome business with a new approach to marketing / Carolyn Tate.
ISBN:	9780730309642 (pbk.)
	9780730309673 (ebook)
Notes:	Includes index.
Subjects:	Marketing — Australia.
	Business enterprises — Marketing.
	Success in business.
Dewey Number:	658.8

Cover design and internal design elements by Spencer Harrison

Printed in Singapore by C.O.S. Printers Pte Ltd

10 9 8 7 6 5 4 3 2 1

Disclaimer
The material in this publication is of the nature of general comment only, and does not represent professional advice. It is not intended to provide specific guidance for particular circumstances and it should not be relied on as the basis for any decision to take action or not take action on any matter which it covers. Readers should obtain professional advice where appropriate, before making any such decision. To the maximum extent permitted by law, the author and publisher disclaim all responsibility and liability to any person, arising directly or indirectly from any person taking or not taking action based on the information in this publication.

To my son Billy . . .
Passionately pursue your purpose, for you have much to offer the world.

CONTENTS

ABOUT THE AUTHOR

Carolyn Tate is the director of Carolyn Tate & Co, an author, speaker and educator, and the founder of The Slow School of Business (Slow School)—a most unconventional business school dedicated to helping small business owners build purpose-driven and prosperous businesses that make the world a better place.

Apart from this book, she has written two marketing books, *Small Business Big Brand* and *Marketing Your Small Business For Dummies* (Wiley); and a personal memoir, *Unstuck in Provence* (www.unstuckinprovence.com).

In 2010, Carolyn sold her house in Sydney, gave away most of her belongings, ended an unhealthy love affair, put her business on hold and escaped with her 12-year-old son, Billy, for an extended sojourn in Aix-en-Provence, France.

On returning to Melbourne in 2011, Carolyn spent her hiatus year working at a not-for-profit before reinventing her business (and life) from the ground up. She is the Victorian Community Leader for Conscious Capitalism Australia and a member of Hub Melbourne, and her company is a Certified B Corporation.

Carolyn is a passionate advocate for the reformation of capitalism, believing that the ultimate purpose of business is to contribute to the elevation of humanity and the planet, with profit being a by-product rather than the single-focus.

As a reformed marketer with 20+ years of experience she's also leading a revolution to reinvent the marketing profession to make it a force for good in the world, starting with this book.

Carolyn also advocates passionately for massive gender realignment and true equality for women everywhere.

To find out more about Carolyn, her speaking services and workshops, and The Slow School of Business, visit carolyntate.co and slowschool.com.au.

ACKNOWLEDGEMENTS

The idea for this book first came about with the publishing of my e-book *The Conscious Marketing Revolution* in late 2012. It was the result of abandoning my marketing business in 2010 and my search for solutions over the ensuing two years on how we might reinvent marketing (and capitalism and business) so it becomes a force for good.

On the verge of releasing the e-book I sought the wise counsel of my loving sister Angela (also an author). I was extremely nervous that I was about to make a public declaration that most marketing and advertising was complete rubbish and contributing to the destruction of humanity. I wasn't sure I had the courage to admit to what I truly believed—especially as I'd made a living for nearly 20 years from this profession!

Her advice? 'Carolyn, dead fish go with the flow.'

It was all I needed to hear. There was nothing more unpalatable to me than being a dead fish, succumbing to conformity and not being able to express my truest beliefs. Within 10 minutes of that conversation I'd sent the paper to my whole mailing list. It was done and there was no turning back.

As small business owners it's hard to swim against the current and stand up for what we believe in. We fear that we'll be considered too left field, too renegade, too opinionated. We fear that it will cost us our reputation, our clients and our future income. The dilemma, though, is that (like many employees in corporate land) we end up doing work we don't love for people we don't love, simply to pay the bills. We lose any passion and sense of purpose we once had. We end up being that dead fish.

A year later, as a result of that paper, I was sitting in the Wiley offices with publisher Kristen Hammond signing a contract to write this book for release in 2014. The delay in publishing was due to the distraction of two other projects very dear to my heart: the completion of my personal memoir, *Unstuck in Provence*, and the launch of The Slow School of Business. Thank you, Kristen, and the wonderful team at Wiley for your patience and faith in me. Thanks also to Jem Bates, my editor, to Spencer Harrison for the cover design and to the other people involved in the production.

Thank you also to my many co-workers and friends at Hub Melbourne, to all the change-making people who come to work and play in donkey wheel house in Melbourne, to the generous and supportive team at Slow School, to the team at Conscious Capitalism Australia and to our volunteer team in Victoria. Thanks also to my family and the many friends who have encouraged me to keep doing the work. And thank you, Billy—the ultimate reason this book had to see the light of day. Unwittingly, each in your own way, you have all inspired me to tap into the resilience, persistence and faith required to keep writing.

Most of all, I want to thank all the dedicated and inspiring entrepreneurs, business leaders and employees of the companies that feature throughout this book (and those that don't)—the free-thinkers and the change makers, those courageous enough to challenge conformist capitalism to make a positive contribution to the regeneration of humanity and the planet.

PREFACE

The beehive and the bees

*The bee collects honey from flowers in such a way as to do the
least damage or destruction to them, and he leaves them whole,
undamaged and fresh, just as he found them.*

Saint Francis de Sales

Perhaps you're wondering what a beehive and bees have to do with a book
on business and marketing?

While many people consider bees a summertime nuisance, without them
our world would collapse. Bees make it possible for many of our favourite
foods, from apples to almonds to pumpkins, to reach our tables. They
transfer pollens from one flower to another, fertilising plants so they grow
and produce food. This cross-pollination gives us 71 per cent of the world's
crops, and more than 90 per cent of the world's wild plants. Without
bees, crops would die and our very survival would be threatened. Bees
are essential for providing bountiful harvests and keeping the human race
healthy. And don't forget the beautiful natural honey they produce for us
all to enjoy.

Honeybees are highly social insects that live together in large, well-
organised family groups. They're highly evolved and engage in a variety of
tasks that serve the needs of their colony, working together for the common
good. They're not solitary like many insects, or like many humans. They
communicate and share the workload and they work in true service to the

collective. Surviving and reproducing takes the combined efforts of every bee, and individual bees cannot survive without the support of the colony.

They also understand inherently that their very existence depends on the continued health of flowering plants. They do no harm to these flowers but leave them whole so they continue to play their part in the delicate ecosystem to which they belong.

Sadly, bee populations are disappearing around the world. Researchers have identified that serious Colony Collapse Disorder is in play. Global warming, pesticide use, habitat loss and parasites are extinguishing the bee colonies and the ecosystems of which they are an integral part.

And that's what's happening in the business world too. Aggressive industry domination tactics, competitiveness and a 'profit at all costs' mindset is causing the destruction of society and our planet.

I want business leaders to learn from the bees — to understand at their core that their business exists to serve their 'colony', the public, and the ecosystem in which they exist. My wish is that companies take an 'inside-out' approach to business by creating products and services that are beautiful, essential and natural; and through attracting the best employees, customers, suppliers and investors, contribute to a better world, thereby rendering marketing as we currently experience it extinct.

My story

> *Man [woman] cannot discover new oceans unless he has*
> *the courage to lose sight of the shore.*
>
> André Gide

A few years ago I was ready to give up my profession for good.

I'd been a marketer for more than 20 years. The first eight of those years were spent in the corporate world working in marketing departments, planning and executing clever campaigns to woo more customers. In 2001, when my first 'mid-life awakening' (a divorce) occurred, I jumped ship from the corporate world to start my own marketing company so I'd have the flexibility to care for my son as a single mother. I wanted to apply the art of marketing to the small business community — a community that really needed help and one that I've come to love dearly.

In many ways I was successful. I wrote and published two books and many thought-provoking articles, ran my own networking events and public workshops, and spoke at conferences all over Australia and New Zealand. I also helped hundreds of business owners engineer and execute marketing plans to grow their businesses. I worked hard, I travelled a lot and I loved my work.

At the same time I was on an incredible journey of spiritual discovery. There was nothing quite like the pressure of running my own business to catapult me into a deeper level of consciousness. I consumed everything I could on personal growth matters and did much soul searching with the help of my counsellor and my ever-growing friendships with like-minded spiritual warriors.

My second 'mid-life awakening' occurred in May 2010. Somehow life just wasn't turning out how it was meant to, despite my spiritual journey. I'd become stuck in so many ways. I was stuck in an unhealthy love affair, stuck with financial difficulty and stuck in a business I no longer believed in or had any passion for. I knew that I needed a drastic change and a major interruption to the stale patterns of my life.

Within months I'd sold the family home in Sydney, given away most of our possessions and was firmly ensconced in Aix-en-Provence in the south of France with my 12 year-old son Billy. I'd become unstuck through one big purge and had no idea what was in store.

While Billy attended the local International Bilingual School of Provence, I took time out from my business, wrote another book (*Unstuck in Provence*), learned a smattering of French (very badly), did yoga, blogged, took up photography and lived a simple, joyful life.

After five glorious, life-changing months, in early 2011 we returned to live in Melbourne. Still unsure of what to do with the rest of my working life, I put my marketing skills to work for a not-for-profit. I thought I'd continue to feel good by doing good for a cause I believed in.

In truth I was buying myself time while desperately attempting to discover my purpose for being on this planet. Mark Twain once said, 'The two most important days in your life are the day you are born and the day you find out why'.

Still racked by confusion around my vocation, I was sceptical that my 'why' day would ever arrive. I've since come to believe that being in a state of confusion is a gift to be cherished, as it forces us to seek out that which will bring us deep fulfilment.

While searching outside (and inside) myself for answers I was becoming more and more aware of how many of the hierarchical structures that make up our society (government, corporations, schools, church, the media) are not serving either humanity or our planet. I joined Occupy marches, read countless books and articles on world issues, watched TED talks and movies, signed up to lobby groups such as Avaaz and GetUp, and joined communities of people on the same journey as me.

I knew inherently that I didn't want my beautiful son to grow up in the world we were all collectively destroying for him.

I was also seeing the role that marketing, my once beloved profession, was playing in contributing to the decay of society. I was ashamed to be a part of the manipulation, the lies, the hucksterism and all the unconscious deceitful practices employed by marketers in both big business and small. I wanted no part of it any more.

It was on the first of May 2012 (two years to the day since I'd made the decision to pack up our lives and move to France for a while) that I discovered my purpose.

I'd just finished reading the ground-breaking book *Firms of Endearment* and was at the launch of Conscious Capitalism Australia in Sydney. Raj Sisodia, an academic and co-author of the book, was the keynote speaker. He made a declaration that literally brought tears to my eyes and caused a physical reaction in my body. 'The 21st Century Marketing Paradigm,' he said, 'reflects a customer centric mindset that turns marketers into healers where our role is to cure, restore health, soundness and spiritual wholeness.'

This single statement caused me to fall in love with my vocation all over again by seeing it through a totally new lens. I knew right then and there that I could lead a revolution to change the marketing paradigm and make marketing a force for good in the world, that I didn't have to give up my profession after all. I could in fact be a powerful catalyst to help businesses market themselves with authenticity, love and compassion, and in a way that would contribute to the nurturing of humanity and the planet rather than its plundering.

Since that day, the most incredible events have occurred. I've connected with the awe-inspiring people at The Hub, a co-working space populated with entrepreneurs creating businesses that are all about doing good while making a profit. I've become the community leader for Conscious Capitalism in Victoria, and a Certified B Corporation. I've held workshops and spoken at events on various topics around marketing and business, and I'm teaching small business owners how to build purpose-driven and prosperous businesses through The Slow School of Business.

And now you're reading the latest manifestation of my purpose, *Conscious Marketing*.

This book is not simply about marketing, though. It's about so much more. It's a call to business leaders, entrepreneurs and marketers everywhere to rethink *why* you do what you do and to discover the incredible capacity of business and marketing to heal our world. Finally, it's a call for us all to join forces to use our companies (big and small) as vehicles for creating a better world for future generations.

About this book

The concepts, theories and opinions outlined in this book are based on my 30+ years of experience (20+ of those in marketing) in both the corporate world and my own small business.

From a professional perspective, they're based on the knowledge I've gained from working directly with hundreds of business owners, reading hundreds of books from change makers in the business and marketing world, watching countless TED talks, connecting with thousands of businesspeople at my events and workshops, attending many non-traditional educational programs and conferences, and reviewing (mostly) non-mainstream media sources.

From a personal perspective, I've spent many years working on my own personal growth and spirituality. Without this grounding, everything I've learned about business would have proven worthless and this book could never have been written.

From a political perspective, while I hold no allegiance to any political party, I have strong opinions, so brace yourself for the ride. As you read this book I encourage you to adopt my mantra: 'Question everything and accept nothing at face value', and feel free to agree or disagree.

If you're interested only in hard-core economic and financial theory and the conventional wisdom offered by traditional educational institutions and texts, I warn you now that you may find this book challenging.

If, however, you're willing to accept that the ultimate purpose of business, capitalism and marketing is to heal humanity and the planet, then you'll love this book and find some wonderfully powerful ideas to transform the way you do business.

The book is organised into three parts. Part I focuses on the current marketing model. The opening chapter outlines where capitalism, business and marketing have gone wrong. It's intended to help readers critically consider why the current ways of marketing are broken. Before we can learn a new way, we must acknowledge and question the old way and unlearn what we've spent decades learning. In order to believe that a new way of marketing—conscious marketing—is possible, we first need to define *consciousness*. Chapter 2 explores what it means to be a conscious being, a conscious consumer, a conscious business leader or business owner. How does our personal consciousness and evolution impact the world of business?

In Part II conscious marketing is introduced and analysed. If we believe that consciousness is the way forward personally and professionally, we can now explore what the idea of conscious marketing might mean for companies.

Part III introduces further ways to apply these new ideas practically. In chapter 9 I outline 10 fundamental shifts to transform marketing from an unconscious activity to a conscious one. I introduce concepts and provide examples of how companies can move from *interruption* to *attraction* marketing, from *complexity* to *simplicity*, from *duplicity* to *honesty*, from *competitive* to *collaborative*... and more. In chapter 10 I demonstrate how to pull it all together into a very simple plan following the Conscious Marketing Map. And I offer you some practical ideas on how to get started and make it a reality in your business.

The Conscious Marketing Manifesto presents a three-page public declaration on how a traditional marketing model can be changed to one that becomes a force for good in the world. It's designed as a reminder for you to refer to regularly as you go about your business and market your services to the public.

Finally I provide a list of further resources, including books, articles, videos and websites, to review and study to help you reinvent your business and your marketing.

Your learning has just begun. Read on!

PART I
The current state
of marketing

Chapter 1
The problem with marketing

Doing well is the result of doing good.
That's what capitalism is all about.

Ralph Waldo Emerson

Oh, if only this were true!

Capitalism is good. It's just that capitalism as we currently know it, is sick and destructive and doing more harm than good to humanity and the planet. Profit is the holy grail of capitalism and it's creating a sick and unhealthy world for our children and future generations to inherit.

It's simply astounding that, according to Oxfam, the world's 100 richest people could alleviate world poverty, not just once but *four times over*. In America, *The New York Times* reports that Wall Street bankers can pay themselves $91 billion in bonuses when thousands of people living on poverty wages are being cast out of their homes for being unable to pay the mortgage.

The stakeholders that always win in this game of capitalism are the executives, board members, shareholders and banking analysts, and the self-serving financial institutions that make them dance like puppets. The stakeholders that lose every time are the customers, the staff, the suppliers—and of course broader society and the planet.

Capitalism has created a competitive, dog-eat-dog, 'you or me' world instead of a 'we' world. For one stakeholder to win, others must lose.

The single-minded pursuit of profit has turned institutions and the people who run them into sociopaths. There's a cancer in capitalism that's destroying our world. While it might be 'legal', it's morally and ethically untenable.

If we're going to create a better world for our children, one that truly puts humanity, love and compassion before personal wealth building, power and ego, we'll all have to do our bit to change our own corner of the world.

Conscious marketing is based on the principle that a conscious approach to capitalism and business must prevail.

Marketing is broken

Like capitalism, the world of marketing (and its subset *advertising*) is deeply broken. It's made us sick, sad, fat, lonely, dumb, numb, stressed, wanting and broke. It's created a society where shopping and accumulating stuff is our daily priority, but the more we consume, the more we need to earn and the more complex and unhappy our lives become.

Today's media bombards us with insidious messages designed to make us all hungry, acquisitive and competitive. It's all about having more—more money, more possessions, more beauty, more assets, more of everything. We've been sold the monumental lie that 'more is better', but that there's simply not enough to go around so in order for *me* to have more, *you* must have less.

We've been sold the monumental lie that 'more is better', but that there's simply not enough to go around so in order for *me* to have more, *you* must have less.

Marketers and advertisers have overrun our environment, thrusting their commercial graffiti into our faces at every opportunity in order to manipulate us into buying. There's simply no escape; from the minute we wake up to the minute we go to bed, we're bombarded with it.

While the number of media channels has increased tenfold, the quality of the message seems to have regressed in direct proportion. In any given day we receive more than 3000 marketing messages (that's two per minute). Is it any wonder that people are tuning out and turning off? And if we do tune in, most of what we are fed is predicated on fear, greed and lies whose objective is to manipulate us to buy stuff we don't need. While attacking the competition, advertisers treat us as though we're idiots, making bland promises they simply can't deliver on.

As consumers (an odious word introduced into our language by marketers), we're the victims of unconscious binge marketing. When marketers need to sell more stuff, they simply turn up the volume and frequency of their promotions, adding to the already over-polluted marketing environment.

It feels like everyone is shouting at us.

According to media education website Lessonbucket, it was estimated that in 2011 nearly $500 billion was spent on paid advertising across the world. This figure is expected to reach well over $600 billion in 2015. Multiply that by 10 (very conservatively) to take into account the real cost of the total marketing industry (including the costs of agencies, marketing departments, website development, database systems, printing, search engine optimisation, video production, direct mail and so much more) and you'll understand just how massive this industry really is. Trillions of dollars are spent on promoting, pushing and shoving products and services into our faces.

The overall return on investment, in financial terms, is anybody's guess. The ROI in human terms is far more evident. In short, marketing is contributing to the decay of society.

The marketing model is broken and drastically needs an overhaul. But there is a better way: it's called conscious marketing, and it's what this book is all about.

Before we learn about this brand-new approach to marketing, however, we must lift the lid on what's truly broken in the current model and understand why it's in the precarious state it is. Only then can we unlearn what we've been conditioned to accept both as citizens and as marketers.

If you're a CEO, corporate marketer, entrepreneur, business owner, ad agency professional or marketer (which is probably most of us), this book

> It's time to change the marketing paradigm, to reinvent it as a force for good in the world.

is for you. If you're a citizen who buys stuff from these people and their companies, this book is also for you. It will inspire you to think twice before you redirect your hard-earned cash to companies that adopt unconscious and harmful business and marketing practices.

It's time to change the marketing paradigm, to reinvent it as a force for good in the world. *Viva la (marketing) revolution!*

Marketing has been hijacked

Advertising. Selling. Promotions. Campaigns. Social media. Websites. PR. These are the words that define marketing in today's fast-paced business world.

The old definition of marketing was all about the 4 P's—having the right *product* at the right *price* in the right *place* and finally ensuring it was *promoted* effectively. Advertising, selling, social media, PR—each was just one part of the promotional mix, not what people today believe to be the definition of 'marketing'. Today that final P, promotion (which includes advertising), drives most businesses. The marketing department's role is simply to promote average products to the masses with smart, creative hooks, using as many media as possible.

Companies and marketers used to take the 4 P's of marketing way more seriously. They used to care about the 4 P's. They used to build outstanding (yet simple) products that truly served their customers and that would make them deliriously happy for the long term. The promotional piece wasn't even considered until the basics of good business and good marketing were taken care of.

For most companies now, good old-fashioned smart marketing is too much like hard work. It's far easier to build a mediocre product fast, add some bells and whistles and discounts to it, and hit the marketplace with a bunch of clever promotions to manipulate people into buying.

Banking is a great example of this crazy notion. Banks by and large operate in a homogeneous, commoditised market with little differentiation between their products, service delivery and online banking facilities. According to a 2010 news article, the Big Four Australian super-banks collectively spend over $1 billion a year on advertising. And don't forget this is just the paid advertising and promotions that can be measured and reported on publicly. It doesn't take into account all the other functions of marketing, such as website builds, mail-outs, PR spin and all the rest of it.

> Marketing as we once knew it has been hijacked by the fourth P, promotion, which is driving most companies in their desperate bid to gain short-term market share and dominate the competition.

A snapshot of the ads of the big banks reveals celebrity endorsements, promotions to spend more in return for more rewards points, competitor bashing and grandiose announcements of the latest banking awards they've won (seriously, who cares!). At a time when public distrust of banks is at an all-time high and executive salaries and company profits are off the charts, these ads do absolutely nothing to endear the public to these institutions. I could certainly think of one billion better ways for banks to spend that money. Could you?

Marketing as we once knew it has been hijacked by the fourth P, promotion, which is driving most companies in their desperate bid to gain short-term market share and dominate the competition.

Marketing for the short term

> *The plans of the diligent lead to profit as surely as haste leads to poverty.*
>
> Proverbs 21:5

Short-termism drives the business world today. Executives demand short-term results from their staff. Shareholders demand the highest possible short-term return on their investments. Banking analysts and stockbrokers rely on the reporting of short-term results to fuel trading from which they earn a very healthy living. Short-termism creates a pressure-cooker business world driven by money, power and competition. It's a battlefield.

And this short-termism directly impacts the marketing of most companies. Short-term campaigns are developed to take advantage of every public occasion imaginable, from end of the financial year to seasonal events, religious holidays, and Hallmark occasions like Father's Day and Mother's Day. Those marketers not driven by the public calendar are driven by their company calendar, a calendar built around their own quarterly financial reporting needs.

Marketers and their extremely obliging ad agencies spend countless hours conceiving clever campaigns to ignite buyer hysteria in order to maximise short-term sales results.

These short-term results may satisfy the executive team, shareholders and banking analysts, but they rarely truly satisfy the long-term needs or even interests of their customers or the public at large. And rarely are these campaigns focused on creating loyal, long-term relationships with customers. They're intended to drive immediate sales — to *fill the till*.

Illogically, they also rarely satisfy the long-term needs or contribute to the long-term profitability of the company.

Black Friday sales across the US show how short-term, quick-profit thinking dominates the retail industry. Black Friday, the day following the Thanksgiving holiday, marks the beginning of the Christmas shopping season. It was originally given the name Black Friday by the Philadelphia Police Force because so many people went out to shop that it caused traffic accidents and outbreaks of violence. 'Black Friday' is certainly not a term of endearment for many American retail workers forced to serve the millions of frenzied and sometimes violent consumers frequenting these sales.

Now retailers have conveniently reclaimed 'Black Friday' as the day that they finally start to turn a profit instead of trading in the red. The combined months of November and December account for up to 40 per cent of retail revenue in the US, so most stores start their discount offers and promotions as early as October.

According to Bloomberg, over the Black Friday weekend in 2013, some 141 million US shoppers hit the stores, spending over $57.4 billion. Yet retail sales still did not meet forecasts, leaving many major stores feeling the pinch and desperate to increase sales with campaigns over the ensuing quarter. And so starts the back-to-school campaigns and any manner of other campaigns to entice shoppers back with their credit cards.

The internet is awash with stories and videos of crazed shoppers battling over sale items they never really needed anyway. It happens in Australia too with the Boxing Day sales.

And to top it off, the mainstream media just loves to compare consumer spending with previous years', as though this is the most vital measure of the health of a nation!

Marketing (and business) for the short term is a crazy notion and it's exhausting for everyone.

The price-war culture

> [A cynic] *knows the price of everything and the value of nothing.*
> Lady Windermere's Fan, Oscar Wilde

Sales. Rebates. Discounts. Giveaways. Guarantees. Price matching. We're constantly being manipulated to buy on price.

Buy today and we'll give you a $2000 rebate on your new vehicle purchase. If you find the same product at a competitor's store at a lower price, we'll match it. Buy this product, trial it for 30 days and if you don't like it we'll refund your money, no questions asked. Sale. Sale. Sale. Today only. Buy two, get the third free. Money-back guarantee.

When it comes to price, the business world has created a monster for itself. Together, with no care and little foresight, they've created a price-war culture in which consumers demand low prices, price matching and discounts. And they've created competitive warfare. In the marketing department all eyes are on the competition rather than on innovation and new, conscious ways of marketing.

And while customers might enjoy the short-term benefit of a lower price initially, in the long run everyone ends up paying the price.

In time, price-driven companies destroy the very stakeholder partnerships they depend on to deliver their products. This includes suppliers who are repeatedly squeezed to drop their prices and staff who are overworked and underpaid and eventually lose their jobs when margins are eroded and the short-term profits start to look shaky. And of course the customer also ends up paying by inadvertently accepting lower quality products and substandard service.

> In the marketing department all eyes are on the competition rather than on innovation and new, conscious ways of marketing.

It would be easy to reply, 'But consumers demand low prices and discounts, so we have to give them what they want'. Well of course they demand low prices, because they've been brainwashed through years of marketing and advertising to expect them.

The price-war culture affects every stakeholder in the chain of delivering a service or product to the market, including employees, suppliers, shareholders, customers, investors and society at large. And of course even our most precious and ultimate stakeholder—the environment—is severely impacted by the price-war culture.

The two biggest supermarket chains in Australia, Woolworths and Coles, are constantly vying to outdo each other and gain market share. When Coles adopted a 'loss-leader' strategy by slashing the price of their own-brand milk to $1 a litre in order to attract more shoppers, the negative impact on the profitability and sustainability of the dairy industry was felt across the country. Then, of course, Woolworths had to up the ante by proposing to buy milk direct from dairy farmers in New South Wales and by striking long-term agreements with them to supply at record low costs. In reality, both supermarkets win in this game. The ones who lose are the suppliers, the farming industry and everyone else dependent on, or enslaved by, these companies.

Sadly, many companies don't see any other way to compete. Price is the only component they have left to manipulate. Consistently and aggressively competing on price is a slippery slide to extinction, however. Withdrawing from the addictive short-term price-war culture won't be easy, but we all must contribute to breaking the vicious cycle.

The mass media minefield

In the old days brands were built on radio, in print and then on television. Consumers (I mean citizens) believed in your company if you could afford to advertise in these media. It was an easy choice and an easy job for marketers and ad agencies.

Today the range of media has increased tenfold. TV. Billboards. Supermarket shelves. Buses. YouTube. Taxis. Airports. Train stations. Bus shelters. Magazines. Papers. Websites. Facebook. Twitter. Pinterest. Cinema. LinkedIn. Google. Emails. Yellow Pages. Online directories. Direct mail. Letterbox drops. Events. Exhibitions...Shall I stop there?

Exhausting, isn't it?

For marketers with money, it's not an easy choice. That's why media buying companies are doing a roaring trade. They're paid to work out where potential customers are lurking, what they're reading, who they're following on Twitter and where the client is most likely to get the biggest bang for their buck. They develop a strategic and comprehensive media plan in order to systematically put the message in front of as many potential customers as possible. Most companies with the big bucks (and particularly those with average, undifferentiated products) will use this 'intelligence' to spread the message far and wide in an effort to cover all bases.

For marketers and small business owners without big marketing budgets, choosing the right medium is an even tougher decision. Without the expertise, time or resources to invest, it becomes a case of trying everything that's free, or at least low cost, to see what works, so they attack the marketing task using a scattergun approach. They try Facebook and Google Ads for a while, and when that doesn't work they try a little email spamming or unsolicited texting, or they buy a direct mailing list or take up cold calling with a vengeance. They end up wasting precious time and money on stuff that simply doesn't work and they're constantly going back to the drawing board to find the next bright shiny way to market themselves.

> What is your purpose? Why do you do what you do? How do you make a real difference to the lives of your clients? What is so good about your business, your service and your products that clients really love you?

A year or so ago I was at a breakfast with a group of small business owners in the professional and financial services sector. Each person was asked to introduce themselves and state where they needed help in their business. One of the attendees made this declaration:

My name is Ken. I'm a mortgage broker. My problem is marketing. I desperately need more business leads. I have about 600 clients and I've tried every trick in the book to drum up some new loans from them and nothing seems to work. I do quarterly newsletters, send Christmas cards, send blogs and invite them to our events. I'm running out of ideas. Can anyone help?

I took a deep breath but remained mute while the rest of the group dished out a whole range of ideas he could try to market his business—tweeting, direct mail letters, free consultation certificates, a mobile app and more.

When it came to my turn, I suggested that Ken first find out if his clients actually wanted a relationship with him and, if so, what they really wanted and needed from him. What I really wanted to blurt out was this: *Stop being an unconscious binge marketer and treating your customers as merely a means to an end. Start marketing from the inside out. What is your purpose?*

Why do you do what you do? How do you make a real difference to the lives of your clients? What is so good about your business, your service and your products that clients really love you?

Whether we're a big corporate marketer or a small business owner, collectively we've become unconscious binge marketers by seeking to spread our message as far and wide as possible using as many media as we can get our hands on. And it's all contributing to an unhealthy, polluted marketing atmosphere.

The manipulative message

We all know that ads sell far more than just products. They sell unattainable ideals, false hopes and utopian dreams. They're designed to manipulate us into believing that we can be thinner, sexier and happier, but only if we open our wallets and buy. They portray images that reinforce who we think we are, or who we think we should be according to mainstream society's conditioning and the mostly untested assumptions of marketing departments and ad agencies around the world.

Ads are designed to manipulate every demographic—men, women, children, families, young and old. Marketers are becoming cleverer at working out what buttons to push in children so they will browbeat their parents to buy the product. This manipulation of children even influences the marketing of products such as cars and holidays that would normally be the decision-making domain of adults.

Ads directed at women perpetuate the insidious myth that their most important asset is their looks. They tell us what the ideal woman should look like and what they should wear. The women in these ads are primped and primed, filmed, photographed and photoshopped, to a point where they become almost unrecognisable. These ads have created generations of women obsessed with their weight, looks and figure.

Women (most often next to naked) are also commonly used and abused in ads targeted at men. They can be found draped over cars, handing a man a beer and bouncing around on beaches. It's ridiculous that this type of advertising continues to fill our screens and magazines. While it might sell a few products by engaging a mainly male audience, the collective damage it does to women's self-esteem is tragic.

The Dove Real Beauty campaign offers an interesting case study. An effort to reverse the negative impact of advertising on women, the campaign was designed to highlight the disconnect between how women perceive their own attractiveness compared with how other women see them. A number of women were asked to describe their facial features to a forensic scientist who cannot see them. He sketches them according to their description. He then asks another person to describe the same woman and he completes another sketch. The result is two very different sketches. The likeness produced from the other person's description is of course much more attractive than the sketch produced from the woman's own description.

It's a powerful and emotive ad that, at least on the surface, helps women feel better about themselves and to accept that they are more beautiful than they believe. But dig a little deeper and you'll understand the hypocrisy of advertising even here.

Dove is owned by Unilever, which also owns Ace and is responsible for manufacturing Lynx men's personal care products. The Lynx ads unashamedly and repeatedly objectify women to the point that some ads have been banned. Unilever also owns Fair and Lovely, a line of skin-whitening products sold in India, South-East Asia and the Middle East. I think the ads for these products are borderline racist, showing the rejection and humiliation of dark-skinned people and promoting fair skin as the secret to success.

While the people responsible for the marketing of Dove may believe in their work and their message, and are applauded for their creativity, put in this context, it suggests that it's all just a clever stunt to increase sales. (Dove sales apparently skyrocketed 700 per cent in the UK as a result of the campaign).

There's no escaping the fact that ads are designed to manipulate us into buying through selling false hope and ideals. Every trick in the book is used to make the product appear desirable. Ensuring your marketing message is honest and ethical and presented with integrity is not an easy task, but it can be done.

A short intervention

By now you may be thinking that my message is all doom and gloom and that I have no faith in marketing and advertising at all. Perhaps we should just ban it altogether and return to the old ways of trading where people just turned up in the market square and sold a goat for a few sacks of potatoes?

I don't think like this at all. I do believe in capitalism and I do believe in marketing. I just think it all needs to change, drastically. This section of the book aims to agitate and provoke, to create controversy and conversation. It's intended to help us all consider why marketing is broken and to grasp that it's possible to view it through a conscious and human lens rather than through a merely financial lens. So please keep reading. Question my observations and feel free to agree or disagree!

The gap between the marketing promise and the customer experience

American author and consultant Roy Williams proposes that 'the first step in exceeding your customer's expectations is to know those expectations'. Sadly, this is the very reason many businesses fail: they make false assumptions about what customers expect and then serve up marketing messages that miss the mark. Or worse still, they actually do understand what customers expect and they make false marketing promises knowing they can't deliver.

While the marketing message may promise that your life will improve tenfold if you buy your shoes from a particular department store, get a loan with a particular bank or purchase your internet services from a particular telecommunications company, too often the exchange leads to disappointment.

The marketing promise turns into a lie once people buy. They discover the product is substandard, the quality of service delivery and the customer experience is poor, or the marketing message has created such unrealistic expectations that they're bound to be disappointed no matter what. Buyer's remorse creeps in and bad word-of-mouth is the result.

There is often a massive gap between the marketing promise and the delivery at the coalface. This gap occurs when management, the marketing department and ad agencies are disconnected from their customers, and incidentally all other stakeholders in the supply and delivery chain. They pursue a top-down approach to business that puts them at the head of a hierarchical structure with too many chains in the link. Break one link and you know the result.

Imagine what messages might be conveyed if executives, marketers and advertisers were to spend real time in the trenches, watching, living and breathing the experiences being provided to their customers, and standing in the shoes of their employees. If they did, would they even consider serving up half the rubbish they put to air?

Companies make too many assumptions about what the customer really wants or they make decisions based on 'market research' that is very often fundamentally flawed. Most research reports are not worth the paper they're printed on and very often they are not used effectively to make any significant improvements, despite what customers might be reporting. In reality, external market forces (mostly financial), politics and competitor pressure are far greater influencers of marketing than any customer will ever be.

The real estate industry demonstrates this very well. A few years ago when I was selling my home in Sydney, I was diligent in my research to find an agent who would respect me and best meet my needs. I asked around for a referral and studied the local paper and finally invited three agents to tender for my business. Of course all three agents talked themselves up as the best in the local area, offered references from satisfied clients and showed me lists of sales results they'd achieved over the past couple of years. In reality,

> External market forces (mostly financial), politics and competitor pressure are far greater influencers of marketing than any customer will ever be.

none of them were differentiated in any meaningful way. They spoke the same language, had identical personalities and approaches, and offered much the same service. Pricing was their only point of difference, with regard to both their projection of how much my home was worth and their fees. It was an extremely tough decision to make and I was uncomfortable with my options. In the end I chose the agent who seemed nice enough and who proposed both a sale price and a commission rate in the mid range.

From the beginning the agent had talked the sale price up, then gradually over the course of the sale period he kept hinting to me that I might have to settle for less. The week before the auction he had emailed me to let me know there were four interested parties and that they had all indicated how much they felt it was worth — all way below my line-in-the-sand price, the one I'd been led to believe I could expect. It took many hours of debate with the agent and the involvement of my father (an ethical real estate agent) to help me through this torturous experience. Despite the agent's duplicity, with my father's support and my own deep resolve not to be duped, we ended up with an acceptable price.

When the marketing message results in a dissatisfying experience, companies are at extreme risk of destroying any respect they may have won from their customers and, more broadly, their reputation in the market.

The sick language of marketing

Talk to any seasoned marketing professional and you'll hear words like *consumer, target market, prospect, market penetration, brand awareness* and *ROI* (return on investment), among many more.

The problem with most marketing parlance is that it's dehumanising. The language causes marketers to think of people not as human beings with real human needs, but as a resource of potential consumers to be manipulated into parting with their money. The task of marketing becomes a left-brain, 'control and numbers' exercise instead of a human exchange.

When we think of people only as consumers, we are removed from the real impact our product or service has on their lives. We don't approach the marketing task with love and compassion. There's no connection between the people responsible for producing and promoting the product and the people buying and using it.

Marketers have an opportunity to think and act in terms of how they can make the customer experience more rewarding, interesting, authentic and real. How can we engage honestly and ethically, without the hype, to help people make good choices, even if that means not buying our product or service?

Imagine how marketing could heal the world if we adopted a healthy language that measures happiness and joy! What if we spoke of 'humans' rather than 'consumers', 'community acceptance' rather than 'market penetration', 'company love' rather than 'brand awareness'?

> How can we engage honestly and ethically, without the hype, to help people make good choices, even if that means not buying our product or service?

Of course we must measure the return on investment for our efforts, and numbers do count. It's just that when they become our sole measure, we risk dehumanising our work and losing sight of the role marketing can play in actually making a difference to the people it's there to serve.

The illusion of choice

'There are three constants in life…change, choice and principles,' so writes Stephen Covey, author of one of my favourite books, *The 7 Habits of Highly Effective People*. I'm really not so sure about 'choice' these days.

Every day we see ads for thousands of different products from apparently competing companies, but the reality is that only a handful of mega-corporations—such as Kellogg's and Johnson & Johnson—control the output and distribution of the world's household brands, from food to clothing.

Did you know that Nestlé (a name most often associated with chocolate) is a $200 billion company that owns nearly 8000 brands around the world, including beauty and clothing brands? Did you know that Procter & Gamble, an $84 billion company, has a reported customer base of 4.8 billion people across the planet and that they're the largest advertiser in the US?

In the US banking sector, 37 companies have merged into just four in under a decade. These companies are JP Morgan Chase, Bank of America, Wells Fargo and Citigroup. In Australia, the Big Four banks account for an incredible 30 per cent of the Australian Stock Exchange value. All of them own other banking brands.

In the media, the story is very similar. In 1983, 50 media companies owned 90 per cent of the US media. Today just six media giants—News Corp, GE, Disney, Viacom, CBS and Time Warner—control 90 per cent of what Americans read, watch or listen to. And in Australia the statistics are even more catastrophic, with News Corp and Fairfax owning 88 per cent of the print media between them.

We're sold the illusion that we have choice, that there's healthy competition in the marketplace, giving us infinite control over our consumption decisions. Fact is, we don't have control. Unless you're a dedicated shopper with the time to research the origins and ownership of every single product you purchase, you simply won't know who you're really purchasing from. That's because the marketing, advertising and packaging will either not divulge this information or, if it is compelled to do so because of some consumer protection legislation, it will be inserted in very fine small print indeed.

These companies are too big to fail and they make the rules. They are the true political power players in the world. If you ever doubted that market collusion occurs, dig a little deeper behind the products you buy. It's nigh on impossible to live a life that avoids these major brands.

Planned obsolescence as a marketing tactic

Our whole economy now is based on the idea that products have a limited shelf life. Ever wondered why the iPhone 6 came out so quickly after the iPhone 5 and the iPhone 4, or why the adaptor-plugs on these phones are different? It's called planned obsolescence, and increasingly electronic gadget and household electrical companies are building this marketing strategy into the production cycle of their products.

Many products are simply designed for the dump. They have a planned shelf life and, incredibly, seem to expire like clockwork. If just one part fails, it can be more costly to replace (if the part is even available) or repair than to buy a new product.

> Many products are simply designed for the dump. They have a planned shelf life and, incredibly, seem to expire like clockwork.

Companies also deliberately omit features, saving them for future upgraded products. Even if the old gadget or product is still functional and does the job very well, marketers lure people into believing they must have the latest version or risk being seen as a social outcast or technologically backward.

Incompatibility is another planned obsolescence strategy. New software A is not compatible with software B, so both must be upgraded to the latest version.

Some months ago I went to get my four-year-old vacuum cleaner repaired at a shop that claimed to specialise in vacuum repairs. The neon flashing sign in the shop window stated categorically: 'All brands of vacuums repaired here'. Within three minutes of taking my Dyson apart, the technician told me it needed a new motor, that he'd have to order it in and that it would take weeks to arrive. He then proceeded to tell me how much it would cost and that even if he did repair it, there'd be no guarantee that the vacuum cleaner would work as effectively as it once had.

After chewing his ear off about planned obsolescence and questioning the ethics of the flashing sign in his window, I got over myself and asked him what he thought I should do. He advised me to buy a new one and assured me that he could dispose of my old one so that the parts would be reused and it wouldn't end up in landfill, which only increased my scepticism.

I weighed up my options. I could take my vacuum cleaner to someone else to fix, buy one from the seconds shop just a block away or buy a new one.

With visitors expected and carpets in serious need of vacuuming, I decided to buy a new one. He showed me the most popular and reasonably priced model in the shop, the one that had been selling like hotcakes. At $500 it seemed like a reasonable buy — until I looked him in the eye and asked him honestly how long I could expect it to last. His awkwardly mumbled yet forthright response was 'three years'.

> Short-term profit is the sole motivation behind planned obsolescence, yet it serves no one in the long term — not the customer, not the planet and, ironically, not even the company.

So now I had another dilemma. Was I prepared to buy a vacuum cleaner that might last just three years while also contributing to landfill with my old cleaner? I surveyed the rest of the vacuum cleaners and turned to him and said, 'Show me a model that will last me 20 years'.

Eighteen hundred dollars later I walked out with a European Sauber with all its carpet-cleaning accessories, a 10-year warranty and a five-year repair guarantee. I felt good about my purchase despite the expense.

Short-term profit is the sole motivation behind planned obsolescence, yet it serves no one in the long term — not the customer, not the planet and, ironically, not even the company.

When CSR becomes marketing fluff

The concept of *corporate social responsibility* originated in the 1950s. Based on the principle that companies should make a positive contribution to society, it's the practice of managing the social, environmental and economic impacts of a company, also known as the 'triple bottom line'. Companies demonstrate their social responsibility through sponsorships, philanthropic activities, community investment, social and environmental reporting and investing in other socially responsible companies.

While the idea behind CSR is a noble one, this strategy has at times been used and abused by many companies. Philanthropy, sponsorships and awards become a PR exercise to distract people from the unethical practices going on elsewhere within and around the company. When a company diverts funds away from suffering stakeholders, including the community and the planet, in order to show their good corporate citizenship through CSR greenwash, then the ethics of that company are questionable.

In many companies, CSR is relegated to the marketing department. Rather than being considered integral to the very fabric of the organisation, it's treated as something that's nice to have and that makes them look good. This renders it inauthentic and often wasteful, except of course to the beneficiaries of the charity. It's a case of robbing Peter to pay Paul.

Here's where the not-for-profit and for-profit sectors are totally disconnected. The NFPs are all about doing good and not about making a profit. They depend on government grants, corporate largesse and public fundraising. The charities' continuing existence is at the whim of funders, except of course when they become 'for-profit' social enterprises in order to secure their own sustainability.

> What if every company or charity had a higher purpose—to do good *and* make a profit?

The for-profit sector, on the other hand, is all about maximising business profits. They leave doing good to the charities and offer them financial support while telling anyone who will listen how socially responsible they are. But the traditional distinction between NFP and FP is outdated. What if every company or charity had a higher purpose—to do good *and* make a profit (see figure 1.1)? Wouldn't that be something?

Figure 1.1: the great divide between the NFP and FP sectors

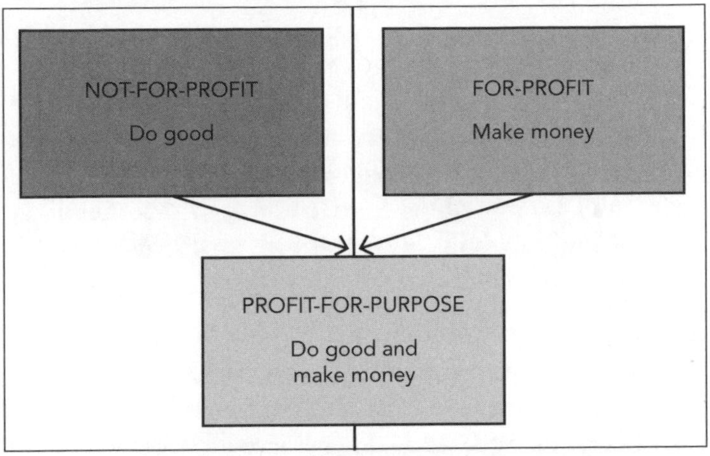

You may be thinking, but at least these companies are doing something good. However, when a company exploits workers, suppliers, the environment and the very stakeholder ecosystem they rely upon for their existence in order to divert funds into external charitable activities, then it seriously lacks integrity. The moral precept that charity really does start at home applies here.

For example, in 2013, Walmart and the Walmart Foundation gave $1.3 billion in cash and in-kind contributions around the world (Walmart Foundation). While this might seem very generous, according to a report from Americans for Tax Fairness, collectively, low-wage Walmart workers are one of the largest welfare recipients in the United States, accounting for $13.5 billion of the $76 billion food stamps issued in that year.

When charity does not start at home, any CSR initiative becomes a whitewashing PR (public relations) exercise. This is the hypocrisy of many CSR initiatives.

The double-edged sword of technology

Clearly, we have many things to thank the advent of technology, the internet and social media for. It has created magnificent opportunities for the disenfranchised, the oppressed and the people who've hitherto had no voice. It has provided a platform for communities to become connected and mobilised to effect positive change in the world. It has helped millions of people to find their soul-mate, to connect with other like-minded communities (think Airbnb and Meetup), to discover new products, services, information and ideas.

Technology has been the great enabler to help lift us out of the broken, capitalistic industrial age and into a new age of empowerment and enlightenment. It has enabled us to think for ourselves and given us the freedom to choose the work we do and who we do it for, whether that's for ourselves or for a small start-up company on the other side of the world.

Yet technology is a double-edged sword.

At a deep personal level, it has contributed to the greatest and most tragic disease of the modern world—loneliness. As Albert Einstein once said, 'It has become appallingly obvious that our technology has exceeded our humanity'.

As traditional social and family structures and neighbourhood communities crumble, people are turning to social media and the internet for connectedness. Sadly, many people exacerbate their isolation through narcissistic behaviour that's all about building brand ME online. They adopt fake personas and endlessly and shamelessly promote themselves to impress thousands of strangers.

Millions of dollars change hands between individuals and companies desperate to learn the tricks of how to build their online brand by massively growing likes, tweets, follows, mentions and ultimately sales. Social media is a great way to grab mass attention, but it's rarely the most effective medium to gain respect.

In short, we've all become tragic self-marketers. It's all about *me*, instead of *we*.

And of course if we reject the latest new social media platforms or trends, we're dismissed as Luddites. The pressure to be on social media 24/7 and constantly plugged in is huge, particularly for youth. Then there's the insidious cyber-stalking, trolling and cyber-bullying that in some cases ends in real human tragedy and death. Of course the same goes for mobile phones and all the other digital devices and platforms that people use constantly to maintain a relentless virtual connectedness.

It's practically impossible for humans to sustain more than 150 meaningful relationships at any one time. And to do this we need real physical, emotional, mental and spiritual human connection. Tragically people spend hours, days, weeks and years locked to their screens instead of connecting in the flesh. While they're more digitally connected and plugged in than they've ever been, many are also as lonely as hell.

And this is where it gets dangerous. This loneliness and emptiness makes people susceptible to manipulative advertising. It makes them more vulnerable to insidious marketing messages and promises of love, health, happiness and nirvana if they buy. Try visiting your Facebook page, watching a YouTube clip or updating your profile on LinkedIn without having an ad thrust in your face. Online marketing feeds expensive addictions like shopping and gambling and is contributing to an unhappy and lonely world. We're all about acquiring things instead of creating and collecting experiences.

We don't yet know the full ramifications of bringing shopping malls to the screens of computers in homes and offices around the world. One thing is for sure: we are social animals hard-wired for physical connection. Spending less time online and more time with the 150 friends, family members and people in your circle of connectedness is the most vital way to contribute positively to the human race and your own little corner of the world.

> Online marketing feeds expensive addictions like shopping and gambling and is contributing to an unhappy and lonely world. We're all about acquiring things instead of creating and collecting experiences.

The great information marketing scam

Over the past decade I've become increasingly alarmed by the thousands of so-called business 'experts' who have flooded the market with get-rich-quick schemes. Information marketing is the process of selling information products, books and programs, both online and offline, at seminars and major events. Information marketers sell their information at public seminars or online with massively manipulative marketing promises.

These products tackle subjects such as how to become a multi-millionaire property owner, how to market your business and attract floods of new clients, how to become a guru in your field in seven easy steps, how to fill your sales funnel and convert customers, how to get ranked number one on Google, how to become a social media guru, how to flee your job and become an entrepreneur, how to work less and earn more, how to dominate your industry and get seen and get heard... and so much more.

While a percentage of them have merit, many are simply white magic.

Marketers toss around advertising headlines like 'get rich', 'maximise your growth and profit' and 'the secret to wealth' to manipulate vulnerable people into believing that if they follow their secret formula, process or blueprint they'll win all the success and wealth they could ask for.

All of these marketers use the 'marketing funnel' approach, with the goal of getting as many people as possible into one room through offering free (or next to free) entry to their events. And while many of them offer interesting and valuable content, they know that most people won't have the skills to employ their wisdom after a day-long seminar.

That's when they employ highly honed 'sell from the stage' skills to persuade a small percentage of punters to part with thousands of dollars. They (literally) bank on the fact that there'll be just enough people desperate for a new life or a new secret key to success to be persuaded. They do the math and they know exactly how many people they can expect to buy into their programs.

When people do buy their products and down the track find they don't actually achieve the promised success, these information marketers claim audaciously that the people simply didn't work hard enough or follow their process. They show little care and accept no responsibility. Conversely, they are very quick to promote the very small percentage of people who do get results (1 to 5 per cent of buyers, if they're lucky). I'd argue these people would have been wildly successful whether or not they'd spent their hard-earned cash on these programs.

The truth is we're all lazy. We get sucked in because we don't want to do the hard and deeply internal, personal work required to identify and fulfil our own personal success paradigm. We don't know our purpose, what we really want out of life (for ourselves, our family or our livelihood), so we let other people define success for us and then we buy into their false promises of nirvana.

Every one of us is unique, with different skills, education levels, values, motives, strengths and weaknesses. It's implausible that one approach or system or process could possibly work for everyone. If you're tempted to participate in one of these get-rich schemes, get out quick and don't look back.

In his book *Outliers*, Malcolm Gladwell suggests an expert needs to have put in over 10 000 hours of practice to achieve mastery in a field. It simply can't be bought like some magic toy from a cereal packet. If you are truly an expert at what you do, then you won't need to market or pitch yourself or buy these dubious programs — you'll have more than enough word-of-mouth referrals to keep you busy.

As a small business owner, marketer, educator and author I've hosted, spoken at and attended hundreds of conferences and events in my time. Having worked in the marketing field with hundreds and hundreds of clients I've earned my stripes as an expert, yet I never refer to myself as one.

> If you're tempted to participate in one of these get-rich schemes, get out quick and don't look back.

I don't feel the need to shout from the rooftops about it or funnel the masses through my programs to prove it. I just work on myself and do my work with purpose, integrity and authenticity. I am courageous in my views and I do not shrink from them, regardless of the opinions of others. I care so deeply about the people I work with that their success, in whatever way they want to measure it, is my success. This gets to the heart of business and marketing. It's about taking all the human pain and suffering and with love and compassion helping people make good, solid decisions about how they want to shape their business so it truly serves their needs and makes a difference in the world.

This idea lies at the heart of a new, conscious era of business and marketing. It's about doing work you love with people you love, in your own unique way, while making a difference in the world.

Native advertising pervading the media

Advertising is the art of convincing people to spend money they don't have for something they don't need.

Will Rogers

Advertorials or sponsored stories have been around for a while in traditional media. They're a cross between an advertisement and an editorial, paid for by the advertiser but framed like a news story. Readers are usually made aware of the fact that it's a paid ad even if it's not blatantly obvious.

Advertorials pop up on the airwaves too, when radio jocks surreptitiously slip in product promotions and endorsements between interviews and stories.

On the surface these ads might seem relatively harmless, but advertisers are becoming ever more cunning, particularly in online media. They're venturing into a new territory dubbed 'native advertising'.

Native advertisers provide advertisements disguised as editorial content or stories. Ads are built into the content or designed to be placed strategically around the content, making it increasingly difficult for readers to distinguish between credible content and clever advertising. Readers can spend a lot of time reading a story before realising it's cleverly disguising a promotion for a product that has creepily been selected for them based on their historical online consumption habits.

It's truly scary what the online world knows about each of us, and scarier still that our critical faculties and our ability to make conscious, informed media consumption choices are being constantly compromised.

My advice? Question everything—or simply boycott these publications.

It seems as though every day some new form of manipulative marketing and advertising technique is being dreamed up. For the consumer in this aggressively over-marketed society it takes real dedication to turn off and tune out. Business leaders and marketers have an enormous and exciting opportunity to be non-conformist and consider how we might do things entirely differently. We live in exciting times. Adopting a conscious approach to marketing a purpose-driven, humanistic business is the future.

Now that I've lifted the lid on how capitalism, business and marketing are contributing to our destruction and why this needs to change drastically, it's time for me to bring a little more positivity to my message. It's time to highlight the very real opportunities that a conscious approach to life and business can bring to our contribution to a better world.

Chapter 2

The evolution of consciousness

The extent of your consciousness is limited only by your ability to love and to embrace with your love the space around you, and all it contains.

Napoleon Bonaparte

Before we engage with the new way of marketing called conscious marketing, we need to define *consciousness* in this context. What does it mean to be a conscious being, a conscious consumer, a conscious business leader or owner? How does our personal consciousness and evolution impact the world of business?

Why consciousness is the key

There are many definitions of consciousness, and countless philosophers have produced hundreds of texts on the topic over the centuries. Consciousness is the quality or state of being aware of what is going on both outside of us and within us. It is about sentience — the ability to feel, experience or perceive subjectively. It means to be awake and alert or

29

compos mentis (having full control of one's mind). It's about making enlightened choices every day, about understanding that the choices we make have an impact on ourselves and that they have a ripple effect.

> It's about making enlightened choices every day, about understanding that the choices we make have an impact on ourselves and that they have a ripple affect.

Of course we can consciously elect to make a choice that may have a negative or a positive impact, yet ideas of negativity versus positivity are highly subjective.

The ultimate stakeholder is, of course, our environment and the planet. In reality, we're all living as though we have three other planets to go to once this one has been used up. In a nutshell, for me, consciousness is simply about having the intent, willingness and ability to *do no harm* — to other people or the planet. It's about making choices that serve others and that make a positive difference.

In today's world, at least in our affluent Western society, we've been manipulated into a collective consumerist mindset. This mindset is ultimately based on the fear that we will never be enough or have enough, that we will always need more in order to 'arrive' and be successful, and that we must have it all NOW!

Corporations, governments, the media and churches have unconsciously colluded in creating a mass unconscious consumerist population who have been brainwashed to accept everything they're told and to question nothing. This mass social conditioning has ultimately dulled our ability to make healthy, positive, life-affirming choices. It's a form of mass control that is, in its outcome, not so different from the kind of absolute tyranny based on fear and violence that has been perpetrated by dictators and autocrats all over the world throughout history.

Just walk through any shopping mall displaying luxury consumer brands to see the blank look on the faces of people looking for the next way to use their credit card to fill the hole in their heart. Of course this hole is also being filled by the pharmaceutical companies who make a killing (literally) with their extensive range of anti-depressants and prescription drugs.

Closer to home, we parents also have much to answer for. Most of us are not demonstrating to our children how to make conscious healthy choices through our own behaviour. We're not having the dinner-table discussions that might help them become more conscious and mindful of the effects their choices have. Meanwhile our children must negotiate the inadequacies of a broken education system that teaches them to compete aggressively rather than collaborate, and to focus on misguided definitions of success attached to academic achievement and career choices.

Today we value money and things more than time, people, experiences, nature and our planet. The root cause of the tragic deterioration of our world is our collective unconsciousness. We haven't elevated ourselves to the highest state of self-actualisation and enlightenment. As Albert Einstein once said, 'No problem can be solved with the same level of consciousness that created it'. So nothing short of a mass shift in our collective consciousness will save us. Something's gotta give, drastically and quickly, if we're to survive.

The conscious being

But take heart! Things are changing, perhaps not as rapidly as they need to, but they *are* changing. As we emerge from the old-world industrial age and into the new 'human' age, millions of people are starting to recognise that they've been unconscious, which is in itself, of course, the beginning of the rise of personal consciousness.

The cause of this awakening is personal pain. As a result of the complexity of life, our overwhelming stress levels and high attachment to materialism, we're suffering now in ways we never have before. Divorce, loneliness, addiction, death, job loss and so many other traumatic life events are causing millions of people to seek radical life changes, to enter the path to enlightenment.

We're asking ourselves different questions. What is my purpose? Why have I been put on this earth? What is broken in the world that I care about and that needs fixing? How can I make a contribution to fix it? How can I *be* the change I want to see in the world? What legacy do I want to create for my family and future generations?

> We're asking ourselves different questions. What is my purpose? Why have I been put on this earth? What is broken in the world that I care about and that needs fixing?

In our search for meaning we're consuming self-help books and spiritual texts with an unprecedented hunger. Inspiring works such as *The Artist's Way* by Julia Cameron, *A New Earth* by Eckhart Tolle and *Man's Search for Meaning* by Victor Frankl have sold millions of copies and been translated into many languages. Millions of people have been brought to consciousness through Alcoholics Anonymous and other 12-step programs. This consciousness and spirituality is happening in spite of, rather than because of, traditional religious institutions. It feels like we have a twenty-first century Renaissance on our hands.

In *Liberating the Corporate Soul*, Richard Barrett (building on Maslow's hierarchy of needs) suggests that all human actions attempt to satisfy one of four needs, physical, emotional, mental or spiritual; and that these needs correspond to one of nine basic human motivations (see table 2.1).

Table 2.1: Richard Barrett's relationship of human needs to personal motivation

Human need	Personal motivation
Spiritual	9. Service
	8. Making a difference
	7. Meaning
Mental	6. Personal growth
	5. Achievement
Emotional	4. Self-esteem
	3. Relationships
Physical	2. Health
	1. Safety

In the first five levels of Barrett's model, we're firmly focused on having our personal needs met and we tend to be inward-looking. As we get past the achievement stage, where often some personal crisis occurs, we seek personal growth and a journey into self-knowledge, which directs us outward towards a search for meaning and desire to be of service to others. As we evolve towards fulfilling our spiritual needs, making a difference and being of service are what matter.

While personal internal forces or trauma are often the first stepping-stones to consciousness, there's another force at play that's helping move people faster up the rungs of consciousness. It's the external forces that are like a hammer to the head. It's the governments, institutions and industry colluders themselves, those with a vested interest in keeping us unconscious.

While focusing their efforts on a divide-and-conquer strategy, these elite groups are increasingly generating massive public distrust and anger as they continue to widen and cement the great divide between the haves and the have-nots. This distrust and anger is being fuelled by the unprecedented transparency offered by social media and citizen journalism.

The internet and social media, and the platforms they are providing, are

Literally hundreds of large and small movements and organisations dedicated to the promotion of regenerative capitalism are springing up...

shining a light on unethical and immoral institutional practices. We're witnessing a new and far broader political awareness through the advent of organisations such as Wikileaks, Occupy (a dispersed movement that has mobilised millions of disenfranchised people in more than a hundred countries and in thousands of cities and communities) and Avaaz (a campaigning community with nearly 35 million members dedicated to bringing people-powered politics to decision making worldwide).

Literally hundreds of large and small movements and organisations dedicated to the promotion of regenerative capitalism are springing up, such as B Lab, B Team, Conscious Capitalism and the Global Alliance for Banking on Values, to name a few.

And layered above all of this, and most likely in the heart and belly of the new world order, is the imperative of a massive gender realignment through which women will play a leading role in reforming the sick and oppressive institutions controlling our world. The rise of the feminine to balance the masculine, harmonising the yin and the yang, is a dream that millions of women and enlightened men foster.

If we want our children and their children to live in a healthier world than the one we and previous generations have created for them, we all need to free ourselves from our own personal bonds so we in turn can become activists and make change happen. We must all take responsibility for raising ourselves up through the stages of consciousness towards a life of service.

Perhaps you're thinking, well that's all well and good, but how can I do this? All I can say is that if you're even asking yourself this question, it means you've started your journey. When you're truly ready, your 'teacher' will appear in many possible guises — through a chance encounter with a like-minded person, through joining a conscious community or participating in a conference, while reading (check out the resources at the back of this book) or watching online programs, or even after joining a 12-step program.

The conscious consumer

Lynne Twist writes in *The Soul of Money*, 'What became clear was that when people were able to align their money with their deepest, most soulful interests and commitments, their relationship with money became a place where profound and lasting transformation could occur. Their money—no matter what the amount—became the conduit for this change'.

These words have rung true for me ever since I attended the Conscious Capitalism Conference in San Francisco in 2013. It was an inspiring two days spent listening to some of America's greatest business leaders, including John Mackey of Whole Foods Market and Raj Sisodia, academic and author of *Firms of Endearment* and *Conscious Capitalism* (both founders of Conscious Capitalism).

At the conference, we explored why capitalism, in its current form, is broken and why it must be reinvented to ultimately contribute to the elevation of humanity and the planet. We heard brilliant speakers talking about why 'higher purpose' must be at the heart of every organisation, and how conscious leadership and a conscious culture have the power to change the face of capitalism, thereby contributing to a rich stakeholder ecosystem in which everyone wins, including the planet.

I learned so much, made some valuable connections and was able to bring back many new ideas and ways of thinking to integrate into my own company. During the two days, however, I was personally experiencing a growing sense of unease within myself and I couldn't put my finger on why.

At the end of the two days we were given an opportunity to participate in a workshop with the Drucker Institute (Peter Drucker's legacy) to help us determine the one visionary thing we were going to do differently as a result of attending the conference.

We were asked to create our own model using Lego, pipe cleaners, paper, stickers and all sorts of items as a reminder of that one commitment we were going to make.

As I closed my eyes for a few minutes to reflect on all I'd learned, the reason for my uneasiness hit me. If I was going to be a conscious capitalist, then I also had to become a far more conscious consumer. So I created this little Lego statue with a woman (me) on top with a coin in one hand and a green leaf in the other.

When *consumers* become *citizens*, making conscious and ethical purchasing decisions by voting overwhelmingly with our hearts, minds and wallets, then unconscious businesses will either die or be forced to innovate and create sustainable, ethical products and services that make the world a better place.

I understood that while I'd made significant inroads in my consumption habits, I had a long, long way to go. I realised that the most significant way I could contribute to changing the face of capitalism was, first and foremost, to become a conscious consumer by spending my money more mindfully.

Today that figurine still sits on my desk to remind me daily of my continued commitment to making conscious and ethical purchasing decisions. It also serves as a reminder that capitalism will change only when we refuse to behave as consumers. When *consumers* become *citizens*, making conscious and ethical purchasing decisions by voting overwhelmingly with our hearts, minds and wallets, then unconscious businesses will either die or be forced to innovate and create sustainable, ethical products and services that make the world a better place.

And this is not just about buying locally grown organic foods or buying recycled clothes and household goods on eBay or at your local charity store. It extends to the service providers we choose, the financial institutions, law firms, accounting firms, consulting companies, creative agencies and so on. Many of these industries are themselves broken and are not set up to serve their clients, or indeed themselves (law firms that charge in six-minute increments, for example). Thankfully there's a growing number of service providers who have recognised this and are operating in a new way. By supporting these ethical and conscious service providers we'll ensure their growth and help them lead whole industries into new conscious territory.

The Soul of Money was a life-changing book for me that put an end to many years of fear around the fact that I never seemed to have enough. The book proposes the idea that money is a form of energy, a currency that flows in and out of our life that is in fact not meant to be 'banked' up. Lynne Twist discusses the idea that the ways we acquire it, use it and share it can be the greatest determinants of our happiness and wellbeing.

Coupled with this is the rise of the gift economy (almost like a return to bartering) that's being championed by leading thinkers such as Charles Eisenstein; technology-driven exchange systems such as Bitcoin, a peer-to-peer payment system and digital currency; and alternative capital raising options through technology-driven crowd-funding platforms like Pozible and Kickstarter.

> We must evolve. We have no choice. And the beauty is that as each of us evolves, so must the world of business!

For many of us, the idea of becoming a dedicated conscious consumer can seem overwhelming. You might be thinking, I'm keen but I have no idea where to start. It's an evolution not a revolution. It starts with small steps and many questions. Has this product been tested on animals? Where was it produced and who had a hand in making it? Does my bank invest in gambling, tobacco or mining companies? Does this law firm charge differently, and do they really care about me? And so on. Have some fun around it with your kids or other household members. Do one thing each day or each week to make a change. Use a KeepCup for your coffee. Stop buying bottled water in your household. Ride a bike instead of driving.

We must evolve. We have no choice. And the beauty is that as each of us evolves, so must the world of business!

Conscious Capitalism

While the industrial age has delivered remarkable achievements and prosperity for many, it has also produced grotesque disparities in wealth. How can it be that one-third of the world's population is overweight, while one-third suffers immense poverty and hunger? How can it be that 30 per cent of the food being produced in the world is actually dumped or allowed to perish, contributing to massive greenhouse emissions, while many millions have nothing to eat?

The corollary of conscious consumerism is conscious and regenerative capitalism—the idea that capitalism can reverse the damage that's been done to humanity and the planet and actually help them to flourish again.

Conscious Capitalism espouses the idea that capitalism exists to elevate humanity and that companies that pursue a higher purpose to serve the greater good will be the most profitable and sustainable organisations of the future.

Conscious Capitalism is also the name of a not-for-profit organisation

The corollary of conscious consumerism is conscious and regenerative capitalism—the idea that capitalism can reverse the damage that's been done to humanity and the planet and actually help them to flourish again.

that originated in the US and now has chapters in a number of countries, including Australia. The Conscious Capitalism movement partners and collaborates with other conscious movements and companies to promote the message that capitalism must evolve. We're here to help light the fire in leaders and to provide them with the resources and connections to help them make change for the better.

Conscious Capitalism is based on the four pillars of *higher purpose*, *stakeholder orientation*, *conscious leadership* and *conscious culture*, as shown in figure 2.1.

Figure 2.1: the four pillars of a conscious business

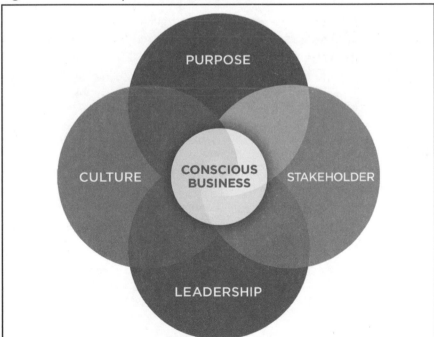

Source: © Conscious Capitalism, Inc.

Higher purpose

Companies that operate with a higher purpose beyond making a profit will be most profitable in the long term. Through engaging all stakeholders in the company purpose, a conscious and caring culture will evolve to ensure that everyone is working towards achieving the company vision.

Stakeholder orientation

All stakeholders play an essential role in the delivery of products and services to the market. Creating value for each stakeholder, whether customers, employees, suppliers, investors, communities or the planet, is at the heart of a conscious company. Like life forms in an ecosystem, healthy stakeholders lead to a healthy business system.

A 2010 global survey by Gallup found that across the world just 11 per cent of employees are actively engaged, 62 per cent are not engaged and 27 per cent are actively disengaged. What is the impact on all the other stakeholders in the ecosystem of having such a massive number of staff either not engaged or actively disengaged?

Conscious leadership

Human social organisations are created and guided by leaders—inspired individuals and managers who see a path forward and are dedicated to inspiring others to travel along this path. Conscious leaders understand and embrace the higher purpose of business and focus on creating value for all and harmonising the interests of all stakeholders. They purposefully activate a conscious culture.

Conscious culture

Culture is defined by Carolyn Taylor of Walking the Talk (a culture change agency) as 'the patterns of behavior that are encouraged or discouraged by people and systems over time. Leaders drive culture, which drives behavior, which drives results'.

Culture is the values, the principles, and the practices that underlie the social fabric of a business, which permeates the atmosphere of a business and connects the stakeholders to each other and to the purpose, people and systems that comprise the company.

There's been little mention of profit in this discussion of Conscious Capitalism. While it's not the driving force or the sole reason for a business's existence, of course profit is imperative in order to continue to do the good work. I believe, however, that we need to shift the conversation away from the notion of profit to the idea of prosperity.

True wealth is about the wellbeing of the whole, which is achieved through the enhancement and harmonisation of all forms of capital—social, ecological, manufactured and financial. Shared prosperity means wealth is distributed equitably (though not necessarily equally) and we have an expanded context of what wealth really is.

Perhaps this idea of 'prosperity for the whole' is a little leftish for your sensibilities, yet there's substantial evidence that the companies that do good massively outperform the S&P 500 over time, as evidenced in the book *Firms of Endearment*.

> True wealth is about the wellbeing of the whole, which is achieved through the enhancement and harmonisation of all forms of capital—social, ecological, manufactured and financial.

The firms of endearment featured in this book have outperformed the S&P 500 14 times over and Good to Great companies 6 times over in a period of 15 years (see table 2.2).

Table 2.2: performance of 'firms of endearment'

Cumulative performance	15 years %	10 years %	5 years %	3 years %
US FoEs	1681	410	151	83
International FoEs	1180	512	154	47
Good to Great companies	263	176	158	222
S&P 500	118	107	61	57

Source: © Raj Sisodia.

US firms of endearment include a basket of 26 'conscious' companies as measured against the S&P 500 and Good to Great companies. These companies include Whole Foods, Panera Bread, Chipotle, Southwest Airlines and Amazon. For a full list and more information visit www.firmsofendearment.com.

The conscious business

If we accept that capitalism must radically change, we could easily be overwhelmed by a sense of futility and the hopelessness of our challenge of effecting change as business owners and leaders.

Alternatively we could consider it an exciting opportunity that offers us a whole new sense of purpose in our business (and life) — an opportunity for immense personal growth, to cease slaving over conventional left-brain competitive and aggressive business thinking, a chance to revolutionise not only our own business but a whole industry.

There are many cases of conscious businesses doing great work, yet in reality not one of them is perfect. Such companies include Whole Foods Market, Southwest Airlines, TuShare, Clearpoint Counsel, Ecocreative, Moral Fairground, bankmecu, Patagonia, The Motley Fool, Atlassian, Pantheon Enterprises, Ben & Jerry's, Intrepid Travel, Whole Kids and Aesop. If you're truly willing to take a deeper look at reinventing your company, a good place to start is to look at what companies like these are doing.

Marque Lawyers: reinventing law

Marque Lawyers is a great example of how a conscious company can be created out of a deep awareness that the industry was failing to serve the needs of either the lawyers or their clients. Michael Bradley founded the company after many years of climbing to the top in corporate law—and burning out. At a Conscious Capitalism conference in 2013, he declared openly that he had everything he'd aspired to as a partner in the firm—the money, the car, the status, the corner office overlooking the harbour. What he didn't have was what really mattered—a fulfilling personal life or any satisfaction from running the company that was chewing up 80 hours of his time every week.

So he abruptly left the company and established Marque Lawyers, a totally different kind of firm. He looked at what was flawed about the practice of law and built a new business model that would address everything the public didn't like about conventional lawyers. Instead of measuring the value of their people in six-minute increments, Marque Lawyers work on retainer. No one has an office—they all work open-plan and move desks every six months so everyone gets to know each other. They have space in their office set up for creatives and artists to use free of charge. They place strict limits on work hours, they play sport together and everyone shares kitchen duties. There is no top-down management structure. They've adopted a wide range of initiatives that have collectively contributed to the growth of their firm and ignited industry conversations.

So how about your business? Start where you are, by asking meaningful questions not just about your own business but about the industry you operate in. Is my industry collectively doing the best for its clients? Is it truly serving all stakeholders? Is it effecting positive change in the world? Or is my company simply conforming in a broken industry? Do I have a higher purpose for the business? Am I being a conscious leader and a great role model? In the beginning you will have many more questions than answers, but that's okay. You don't need to know all the answers. You just need to find the courage and willingness to ask the questions and take the first steps towards making small changes.

> Start where you are, by asking meaningful questions not just about your own business but about the industry you operate in.

The conscious leader

If your actions inspire others to dream more, learn more, do more and become more, then you are a leader.

John Quincy Adams

A conscious company is simply the entity that evolves over time owing to the collective consciousness of the leaders and stakeholders. Without conscious leadership, a conscious culture and organisation cannot exist.

But what does it take to be a conscious leader?

Conscious leaders are evolved and enlightened. They act consistently and diligently to serve the purpose of the organisation and the people charged with delivering on that purpose. Being of service and making a difference is in their DNA.

The reason capitalism has gone so horribly wrong can be attributed to a serious imbalance between the three vital levels of intelligence, outlined in *Spiritual Capital*, a book by Danah Zohar and Ian Marshall, as depicted in table 2.3. The single-minded focus on *material capital*, based on IQ (rational intelligence) and the mind 'what I think', has prevented *social capital* and *spiritual capital* from manifesting adequately.

> Conscious leaders are driven by a *we* mindset rather than a *you or me* or even an *I* mindset.

Table 2.3: the three types of intelligence (Danah Zohar and Ian Marshall)

Capital	Intelligence	Function
Material capital	**IQ** Rational intelligence	What I think
Social capital	**EQ** Emotional intelligence	What I feel
Spiritual capital	**SQ** Spiritual intelligence	What I am

Source: © Danah Zohar 2013.

Thankfully, leaders are beginning to recognise that it's vital to ensure equal measures of rational intelligence, emotional intelligence (which emanates from the heart) and spiritual intelligence (which emanates from the soul). A conscious leader balances IQ, EQ and SQ.

Conscious leaders are driven by a *we* mindset rather than a *you or me* or even an *I* mindset. They display qualities such as patience, vulnerability, generosity, fearlessness, empathy, non-criticism, discipline, peace, modesty, humility, truthfulness, equity and transparency. Conscious leaders seek to restore the imbalance between the feminine and masculine in business. They are real, authentic and human, and are not just respected but loved by their people.

Conscious leaders serve. They don't subscribe to top-down, divide-and-conquer leadership modes. They're willing to adopt new styles of leadership such as Holacracy, in which authority is distributed and governance of the organisation occurs through its people in pursuit of the purpose. Zappos, a successful US online retailer, actively applies the

Holacracy model and others are rapidly following suit. It's a courageous new way of doing business and fulfilling a company's purpose (and financial requirements).

One of the most conscious new leaders to emerge in recent times is Pope Francis. I do not subscribe to any conventional religion (although my thinking tends towards Buddhism), but I see Pope Francis as one of the most enlightened leaders in the world today. There's no doubt that he has one of the toughest gigs in history. At a time when trust in religious institutions is at an all-time low, he's tackling his work with gusto.

He has given millions of people (and not just Catholics) new hope. He's been willing to accept responsibility for the sins of the Catholic Church with regard to their scandal-ridden bank and their cover-ups and hypocrisy around sexual abuse. He has been courageous enough to excoriate the Mafia (towards whom the Church has turned a blind eye in the past). He's denounced the 'cult' of money and admonished the power players behind the financial system. He's spoken out strongly against war-making. He has chosen not to live in the luxurious papal apartments. He's washed the feet of the poor and ill (including non-Catholics), held the children and blessed the animals. He's exhibited the most vital traits a conscious leader can exhibit — the ability to act with humility, admit fault and apologise.

> Finding the courage and vulnerability to admit you can do better and being willing to change and learn are all it takes to get started.

If we're going to see massive change in the world we'll need many, many more inspiring leaders displaying the traits of Pope Francis and others like John Mackey of Whole Foods Market, Richard Branson of Virgin and Tony Hsieh of Zappos. Every leader can learn a thing or two from studying the masters of leadership. Finding the courage and vulnerability to admit you can do better and being willing to change and learn are all it takes to get started.

The conscious employee

If you're an employee becoming increasingly disengaged with your job or the company you work for, ask yourself why. It could be simply that you don't enjoy the job, but it will probably run far deeper than that. It will most likely be to do with the consciousness of your leaders, their ability to lead, and a growing discomfort that your personal values do not match the values of your leaders or the espoused values of the company. Or it could very well concern your own level of consciousness and awareness.

Many years ago I spoke at a conference for librarians in Sydney on the topic of 'verbal branding' and the importance of responding intelligently to the standard networking question *what do you do?* I asked a woman in the audience to stand up and then asked her the question. Her response? *I'm just a librarian.* To cut a long story short, through some mindful questioning I addressed that word 'just' and gently coaxed her into reframing the answer to this question. The new response? *I give the gift of reading to parents, so they can pass it on to their children.*

A couple of weeks later I received an email from the woman telling me that that one conversation was the most transformative experience she'd had in many years. She admitted to me that she'd never considered how vital her job was and had never thought of herself as more than a mere dispenser of books. Clearly her employers had let her down. It took a stranger to help her understand how integral she was to her local library and the community she served.

While one might blame her leaders for not valuing her or ascribing meaning to her work, in truth it is as much her responsibility as theirs. Each one of us can find meaning and purpose in our work if we look deep enough. We don't need to wait for our employers or leaders to give us this sense of meaning at work.

While a conscious leader will inspire their employees to think and act beyond their functional role and help them understand the deeper purpose of their work, a conscious employee will seek this out for themselves and take responsibility for it.

While a conscious leader will inspire their employees to think and act beyond their functional role and help them understand the deeper purpose of their work, a conscious employee will seek this out for themselves and take responsibility for it.

A famous example of this is recorded in a Kennedy story from 1962. When President Kennedy was touring NASA he noticed a janitor wielding a broom, whereupon he allegedly interrupted the tour and walked over to the man and said, 'Hi, I'm Jack Kennedy. What are you doing?' The janitor responded, 'I'm helping put a man on the moon, Mr President'.

In reality, we're all leaders and we're all followers, and titles and hierarchies are barriers to creating a conscious culture. As an employee you can show incredible leadership by modelling the qualities and values you wish to see your managers and executives display. If you do not compromise or act subserviently, and if you take initiative to express your opinions and beliefs with respect and mindfulness, then you will find yourself enjoying your job much more.

If you're finding that your personal values are shifting so they no longer match the values or culture of the company, there's lots you can do. Start by exploring the recommended books and resources listed at the end of this book. Start learning about this stuff and sharing it with others in your company. If you're brave enough, share it with your leaders! Soon it will become clear to you how you can make a positive contribution within your organisation and help lead the company to a greater level of consciousness and contribution to humanity. And if you can't effect change and instead find yourself being stonewalled at every turn, perhaps it's time to start searching for a job at one of the thousands of emerging companies that will give you the respect and consideration you deserve.

The conscious community

As we grow in consciousness and start to turn our attention outward, away from ourselves and towards being of service and making a difference to others, many of us seek out like-minded communities to connect with and belong to, particularly if we feel disconnected from our current work and home communities. We want to be among like-minded souls who share our beliefs and who also want to bring about social change.

During 2011, when I first moved to Melbourne, I had few friends, no family and no community here. I had to start all over again and build my own community, something I'd been quite successful at doing in Sydney. Much of the year was spent studying capitalism, politics, business and marketing, observing the good, the bad and the ugly, writing about all the things that I'd like to change and about how my own business might be a small part of making a difference.

I journaled, wrote poems, papers and blogs, watched countless movies and TED talks, and read innumerable books and articles—I immersed myself in learning. A switch was flicked and my mindset and consciousness were changed irrevocably.

What became ever more apparent to me was that I had very few like-minded friends with whom I could share my thoughts, feelings and learnings. When I did share my ideas they seemed to fall on deaf ears, and the less others listened the louder I got (which must have been extremely annoying for many and likely only served to alienate them). I felt extremely lonely and disconnected and wondered if I was the only crazy one passionate for change.

And that's when many wonderful things happened that brought me to my like-minded online and face-to-face communities—Conscious Capitalism, The Hub and more. I found other people who believed what I believed, a place where I could hear about the good work of literally hundreds of businesses that are doing their best to effect positive change—businesses like Small Giants, Safety Culture, Oursay, Hitnet, Dumbo Feather, The Project Room and Kinfolk Café. I found a community where I belonged and could talk about the important stuff without being ridiculed.

> The process of finding your tribe starts with searching within to become more personally and professionally evolved and aware.

And now, as a result, my clients are of a similar mind and I'm building a collaborative business school (The Slow School of Business, aka Slow School)—a community for like-minded professionals who come together to create positive change through building their own purpose-driven businesses.

When profound change happens within you, it's natural for the old you to fall away and for you to start looking for like-minded communities that share your dreams and ideas. You don't need to feel lonely. Whatever your specific interest or passion, whether it's alternative energy sources, community gardening or political change, there's a geographic or online community that serves it.

The process of finding your tribe starts with searching within to become more personally and professionally evolved and aware. It's also about learning to deal with a degree of discomfort and doing things that are outside your comfort zone. It's about being willing to say, 'Hey, this is not right and I'm going to change it'. It's not about demonising anything or anyone. It's about standing up for your beliefs and taking positive action to bring about positive change.

I hope you've found this exploration of the concept of consciousness thought-provoking and have picked up some ideas to start working with. To become a conscious marketer you must first be willing to become a conscious human being. In Part II we delve into a whole new way of marketing. Read on!

PART II
The reinvention
of marketing

Chapter 3
Introducing conscious marketing

What lies behind you and what lies in front of you, pales in comparison to what lies inside of you.

Ralph Waldo Emerson

If we believe that a more conscious and aware life is the way forward both personally and professionally, we can explore the idea of conscious marketing and what it might mean for you and your business.

As an obviously biased (yet reformed) marketer, I believe that marketing is actually the most essential ingredient to building a conscious business. Marketing is responsible for the way your customers, suppliers, employees and community perceive you. It's responsible for whether these groups are attracted to you, stay with you and tell others about you. No matter how brilliant your business is, without great (and conscious) marketing, it will not fly.

In this chapter I outline what conscious marketing is and offer you a new model to consider: the Cycle of Conscious Marketing. This model is designed to help you rethink your marketing and business and how you approach it, to recognise that marketing is an inside-out job and has the power to transform your company.

Defending marketing

'Business has only two functions, marketing and innovation', suggests Milan Kundera. Deep down, even after all my fault-finding with marketing, I know that he is right and that I'm in fact writing this book to defend and promote my profession, not condemn it. I believe many people don't really understand the value of great marketing. Sadly, it has come to be seen as the 'promotions and pretty pictures' profession, an element to be slapped on once the heavy lifting has been done and the product is about to be flung into the marketplace. The expense involved is accepted reluctantly, rather than being seen as a valuable investment that might ensure the product will actually sell even before it's built.

Recently I was in a meeting with my clients and their lawyer and accountant. We were about to embark on a quite expensive (but necessary) rebranding exercise and the question from the accountant was 'What is the return on investment on this exercise?'.

> I believe many people don't really understand the value of great marketing.

I responded with a list of things we would measure (from customer perception to new website traffic) and talked about the potential cost to the company of not rebranding. I was soon justifying why marketing even needed to exist. Later, reflecting on this little interaction, I found myself quite annoyed. I wondered why this question is tossed at marketers when other essential functions required to run a business, such as legal and accounting services, sales and HR, don't get quite the same grilling around ROI.

When times are tough and budgets need to be cut, guess which is the first to go? Marketing. In many companies, internal competition for attention and funding is actually greater than any external competition. It feels like everyone is pulling in different directions to protect their own turf, and marketing is often treated as the poor cousin.

Perhaps marketers have simply done a bad job for too long and they've learned not to ask the hard questions, to challenge the decision makers and to help make marketing real and meaningful. Perhaps the real problem is that marketers have not been willing to adopt an inside-out view of themselves and of the company and product or service they are being asked to market.

Marketing must be totally reinvented to gain the respect it deserves and get a seat at the boardroom table alongside the CEO. Without solid marketing behind it, the best product in the world will sit gathering dust on the shelves. No matter what our role in the company, we all have the obligation to consider how marketing can be made good again.

Defining conscious marketing

So how do we shift marketing away from being merely about pretty pictures and towards something real and meaningful? We take a conscious approach to it—we practise conscious marketing, making it an inside-out rather than an outside-in job.

Conscious marketing is all about building something so fundamentally good and compelling right into the heart of your business, products and services that everyone (suppliers, employees and community) wants to join your tribe and spread the word.

It's about working out who you really want to serve and then asking how you can best serve them, way before you even start to build the product or service. The old adage 'who cares matters and who matters cares' is key.

Conscious marketing is not about building an ordinary product and then manipulating people into buying it through unconscious and mass-binge promotional activities. It's about building a company, products and services with deep regard for the customer while engaging with, and taking care of, all stakeholders in your ecosystem.

It's about building something so good that it requires minimal investment in mainstream promotional activities.

> It's about building a company, products and services with deep regard for the customer while engaging with, and taking care of, all stakeholders in your ecosystem.

Your business becomes a *movement*, a place where people feel they belong, a conduit for like-minded people seeking to effect change.

Conscious marketing is about ensuring your marketing activities are aligned with your higher purpose—the *why* behind what you do. It's about taking a cause leadership approach and bringing your industry along with you in a spirit of collaboration rather than competition, to address and fix what's broken in your industry and what isn't serving people.

Finally, conscious marketing is about promoting your offering with honesty, transparency and congruency and with messages of joy, hope, love and humanity.

Ultimately your business will be sustainable and profitable because your product or service and your message will make the world a better place. It's about long-term sustainability, where profit is a by-product rather than the single focus.

What conscious marketing is *not* is merely another term for corporate social responsibility or philanthropy. I've already discussed how companies can exploit CSR as mere PR spin even while other stakeholders are abused. With conscious marketing, every stakeholder is loved in the process of delivering a service to the marketplace.

An introduction to the Cycle of Conscious Marketing

Perhaps you're thinking this sounds all well and good but how do I do that? What steps do I follow to make that happen? How do I get started?

The Cycle of Conscious Marketing is my own model developed after years of teaching marketing, writing books, reading texts, and considering what has truly worked with clients and workshop participants and throughout my many years of experience in the profession.

As I step you through each phase of the model, I'll give you some great examples of companies that are adopting conscious business and marketing principles.

At the heart of the model (see figure 3.1) are five core elements: **Personal** (you, represented by the yogic silhouette); **Purpose** (why); **Product** (what); **People** (who); and finally **Promotion** (how), which you will note lies outside the internal circle.

Within each of these core areas a number of considerations come into play, and these will be introduced at the appropriate point.

Figure 3.1: the Cycle of Conscious Marketing

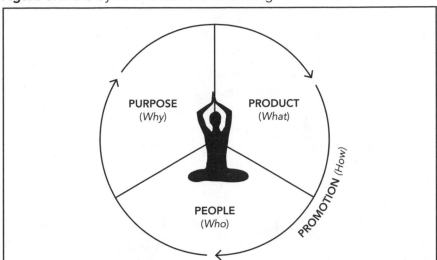

Personal (you)

At the heart of making sound business and marketing decisions is your ongoing hunger for personal growth and development and your commitment to the daily evolution of your awareness and consciousness. Successful business owners and leaders understand absolutely that business success is 50 per cent personal and 50 per cent professional. Without a commitment to personal learning and growth, you may profit in the short term but you'll never achieve long-term success.

Purpose (why)

Purpose is the glue for your business—without it, you have nothing. Purpose is all about *why* you do what you do, about defining at the core what you stand for and how your business will make a difference in the world. All business decisions stem from purpose. Your messages and communications, both internally and externally, align with your purpose or cause. Your company, in effect, becomes a cause leader in your industry. A good place to start with purpose is to ask, 'What's so broken in my industry that it needs fixing?' Then go fix it. While your purpose becomes a clear statement of intent for your business, it's your actions that make it real. Think of your business as a 'movement' rather than a commercial enterprise.

Product (what)

Your products and services are the manifestation of your purpose. Your aim is to build products and services that are so good and so compelling that people simply want to join your tribe. You can never spend too much time on truly understanding who you want to serve and how your product best serves them (this includes every part of the delivery and service experience). Many companies do the opposite. They take the 'build it and they will come' approach and then find themselves using mass promotional tactics to manipulate people into buying. This is the opposite of what conscious marketing theory demands.

People (who)

Of course it's imperative that your product or service is built with your ideal customer in mind, but it must also be built with *every* stakeholder in mind and 100 per cent on board. Think of your business as an ecosystem that embraces that other ultimate P—the planet—alongside your community, your suppliers, your employees, investors, your industry and even your competitors, and finally of course your own family. The leaders of purpose-driven companies practise universal love and humility

> Of course it's imperative that your product or service is built with your ideal customer in mind, but it must also be built with *every* stakeholder in mind and 100 per cent on board.

in the knowledge that they're simply a cog in the wheel of life and business. When every stakeholder is continuously engaged at a purpose level, and when they believe deeply in your product, they'll be your most loyal fans.

Promotion (how)

This is the final element in the equation, the area most closely associated with marketing. While promotion is of course essential, in this model I've placed it outside the integral circle because I believe that if you continuously focus on the other four elements, the promotional activity becomes less crucial to your success and sustainability. The promotional task becomes simpler, and less time-consuming and costly, as new business comes through word-of-mouth and reputation. Promotion also becomes a much more authentic and deeply enjoyable activity because it comes from a deep sense of purpose and service. Chapter 9 outlines 10 fundamental shifts that can lift the promotional activity from unconscious to conscious.

How it works

This model is designed as an unbroken, never-ending cycle that is continuously in motion. Everything, however, stems from purpose, the glue that dictates all decision-making. It's a top-level model that overlays many deeper areas and questions that need to be considered for each element. For example, Purpose (why) is the precursor to defining your vision and values, while Product (what) is the precursor to considering your customer service experience, and so on. Table 10.1 (see p. 172) presents a map you can follow that identifies each of the subsections for each element.

Whether you're a corporate escapee starting out on your own, a seasoned business owner with 20 employees, or head of the marketing department of a major institution, this model can be usefully applied. It helps to consider the model as though you were a start-up, to look at it with fresh eyes. What would you do if you could start all over again?

In the next five chapters we'll examine each of the 5 P's in detail and show them at work in real companies from across the globe. I hope you find them inspiring and are encouraged to study the companies further for inspiration in your own business and life.

Chapter 4

Personal consciousness—an essential ingredient for conscious marketing

The chief objective of education is not to learn things but to unlearn things.

G.K. Chesterton

Many pages of this book have already been devoted to the notion of personal consciousness and what it means to be a conscious leader and business owner. Your dedication to personal growth reflects directly on your business success, growth and sustainability.

So what to consider in the evolution of your personal consciousness and the pursuit of meaning? There are thousands of books and other resources devoted to this subject, some of them are mentioned at the back of this book.

> Your dedication to personal growth reflects directly on your business success, growth and sustainability.

The path to consciousness and awareness is an intimate, private and personal journey. It requires great honesty (with yourself and others), a willingness to face your afflictions and addictions (yes, millions of people have them), courage to continue the journey and the shedding of the old (habits, friends, business colleagues or partnerships, things that don't serve you) in order to embrace the new.

A dedication to learning

'Formal education will make you a living. Self-education will make you a fortune.' So writes American author and educator Jim Rohn, whose own rags-to-riches story proves his point. A dedication to continuous learning that is more informal than formal can mean the difference between failure and success.

In a world awash with information yet very little knowledge, you'll most likely need to empty out your old (and often unhealthy) cup of knowledge and practise real discernment in what you refill your cup of knowledge with. The essential ingredients that guarantee your personal evolution are awareness, intuition, and a dedication to learning and practice.

The world of education, like the business world, is homogeneous and industrialised. Those of us fortunate enough to have gained an education were put through a system that taught us mostly irrelevant content using 'command and control' teaching techniques followed by demands that we regurgitate our learning in standard testing before being graded and pitted against our peers.

This system largely dulled our ability to access our intuition, reasoning, questioning, critical thinking, spirituality and creativity.

The most watched video on TED, Sir Ken Robinson's *How Schools Kill Creativity*, has more than 29 million views. In it, he argues that kids are born with incredible talent and creativity but that our industrialised education system educates it out of them. He believes that creativity is as (if not more) important in education as literacy, and that the arts are treated as a very poor cousin to academia and sport.

The public education system was developed around 1900 specifically to meet the needs of industrialisation. As a result, the whole schooling system came to be predicated on academic ability. Students are steered away from pursuing their creative passions in the belief that they won't ever 'make a living' from them.

The industrialisation of education and the resulting pandemic loss of creativity is a major contributor to the cancer that exists within capitalism. Education will be the great enabler in bringing consciousness to the business world, and it starts with each of us taking responsibility for our own learning. We must adopt new ways of learning in which creativity, innovation, play, connection and collaboration become the foundations.

Thankfully, some traditional educational institutions (although not nearly enough yet) are seriously recognising that the old ways of industrialised education no longer work. They're starting to get curious about new ways of learning, although it will be a long time before widespread change is effected, so don't hold your breath! My own personal enlightenment around education has been very strongly abetted by two young mentees of mine, Simon Harman and Remy Grangien, who have started The Co-Learners, a business directed towards new ways of learning in which students learn from each other collaboratively.

Conscious people most often feel uncomfortable in conventional educational institutions. They learn differently and approach assumptions with a critical, questioning mindset. They're highly creative, they colour outside the lines, think with their heart and are willing to makes lots of mistakes. They hate rules, take risks and dream big.

They understand implicitly that everything before them is their teacher, whether that's a conversation with a business colleague, a documentary, an article, a book, or attendance of a specialist class or discussion group. They choose carefully what goes into their knowledge cup and they turn off the tap that has filled it in the past, such as mainstream TV and the media.

Conscious learners embrace every opportunity to learn. They go to bed reading, they wake up and journal, they listen to audiobooks, they meditate daily, they pray, they are present to every moment. They establish daily learning rituals using the tools that work best for them.

> Conscious learners embrace every opportunity to learn.

All of these learning experiences are like bricks that are built one upon another, helping to guide you to making conscious decisions.

Conscious beings are also incredibly intuitive, and this is where their learning choices stem from. Despite what we've been led to believe, intuition does not involve some divine intervention from above. Intuition is actually the ability to acquire knowledge from insight. The word derives from the Latin verb *intueri*, which means to look inside or to contemplate. As we stack up our knowledge building blocks we are increasingly able to access this intuition. Rudolf Steiner placed intuition as the third of three stages of knowledge, after imagination and inspiration.

I truly don't believe that effective learning can be achieved through the current educational system. We must embrace the new way of learning that's emerging — putting students at the heart of their own education, encouraging self-directed learning with peers using experiential and collaborative learning practices. I believe that the best learning is accomplished slowly, mindfully and purposefully with a tribe that matters and cares and with whom there is equal exchange and deep connection.

That's why I've decided to put my money where my mouth is to launch and curate The Slow School of Business (Slow School). Slow School is an unconventional business school for entrepreneurs and small business owners who want to build a purpose-driven and prosperous business that will make the world a better place. We practise collaborative and experiential learning that covers the emotional, spiritual, practical and rational intelligence skills required to build a successful small business. Importantly, all our people are both teachers and students.

Students are connected deeply to a tribe of people who share a common purpose, and we offer continuous learning classes and continuous connection to the tribe. We're creating a movement in the business education world.

Why 'Slow'? In a world where fast-change, fast-profit and short-term thinking dominate, the Slow movement advocates a cultural change of pace. Speed isn't the answer. Slowing down to a mindful and purposeful pace (not a snail's pace) is the path to a better life and a better world. And this applies equally to the world of learning and to business.

There are now slow living, slow food, slow cities, slow money and slow education movements happening around the globe.

Carl Honoré, in his book *In Praise of Slow*, sums it up beautifully:

> Fast and slow do more than just describe a rate of change. They are shorthand for ways of being, or philosophies of life. Fast is busy, controlling, aggressive, hurried, analytical, stressed, superficial, impatient, active, quantity-over-quality. Slow is the opposite: calm, careful, receptive, still, intuitive, unhurried, patient, reflective, quality-over-quantity. It is about

making real and meaningful connections—with people, culture, work, food, everything. The paradox is that slow does not mean slow. Performing a task in a slow manner often yields faster results. It is also possible to do things quickly while maintaining a slow frame of mind.

If you do nothing after reading this book but develop a deeper hunger for unconventional, self-directed, collaborative and continuous learning, then I'll have done my job and you will be richly rewarded. Get to it!

A reframe of the success paradigm

Somehow, somewhere along the line, our modern world has redefined success in financial, material and social status terms. Somehow success has come to be equated with how much you own, how big your company is, how much profit it makes, how many hours you work, your job title, what you drive, where you live and where you went to school. You can be a complete asshole and run a company that plunders the earth and still be deemed to be hugely 'successful'. Go figure!

Coupled with the imperative to refill our cup of knowledge with the good stuff, is the need for us each to personally reframe our own notion of success and not buy into the success story sold to us by society and the media. By understanding what success means to us personally, we can then consciously choose what we most need to learn and how we can best learn it.

Defining success in your own terms is not easy. For me, success means many things. It means continuously finding the courage to be true to myself so that I may live a life of purpose and meaning. It means living a spiritual and creative life that allows me to play to my strengths (writing, teaching, connecting people, building communities). It means being a wicked role model for my son. It means travelling far and wide while consuming less and as consciously as I can. It means being committed to continuous learning. It means building a business that allows me to bring who I am (warts and all) to the table, to connect consciously with my business community and to make a healthy living from it...and so much more.

Interestingly, when I ask people in my workshops what success means, rarely is the answer about having stuff or making millions. They are always quite humble and simple. Answers commonly include 'spending more time with my family', 'having time to myself', 'unleashing my creativity', 'living in peace and harmony', 'resolving a personal problem', 'creating stronger bonds with my family', 'rebuilding my business so I'm doing work I love with people I care about', 'solving local and global problems' and 'being healthier'. What does success mean to you?

The notion that every businessperson wants fame and fortune is ludicrous. And the same goes for employees. Most people simply want to generate a healthy, reliable income from their work, allowing them to be successful on their terms and thereby lead a wholehearted life that allows them to make a contribution. That's why we all need to pursue our *own* definition of success, rather than the one sold to us.

Fewer than 1 per cent of Australia's 2 million registered companies employ over 200 people and just 4 per cent employ over 20 people. That means the rest of us are either micro or small business operators. That's a huge number! While it might be a cliché, small business truly is the backbone of Australia, as it is in almost every other country. As whole companies and industries collapse as we evolve out of the industrial age and into the human age, and as more people escape the corporate factories to look for greater meaning in their work, this number will only skyrocket. Collectively we'll have a massive opportunity to redefine success on our own terms, to embrace the notion that small is beautiful and that less is more.

Success is as much about *being* as it is about *having*. It's about living by your personal manifesto—a public declaration of your intentions, beliefs, views, motives and actions. It spells out your philosophy on how you wish to live your life. It identifies how you mean to behave in order to do what needs to be done and to achieve what you want to achieve. The Holstee Manifesto (see figure 4.1) is one famous example of a manifesto that has inspired hundreds of thousands of people around the world. My own personal manifesto (see figure 4.2, p. 66) sits in a frame above my desk. The Conscious Marketing manifesto can be found at the end of this book.

> Success is as much about *being* as it is about *having*. It's about living by your personal manifesto—a public declaration of your intentions, beliefs, views, motives and actions.

Figure 4.1: the Holstee Manifesto

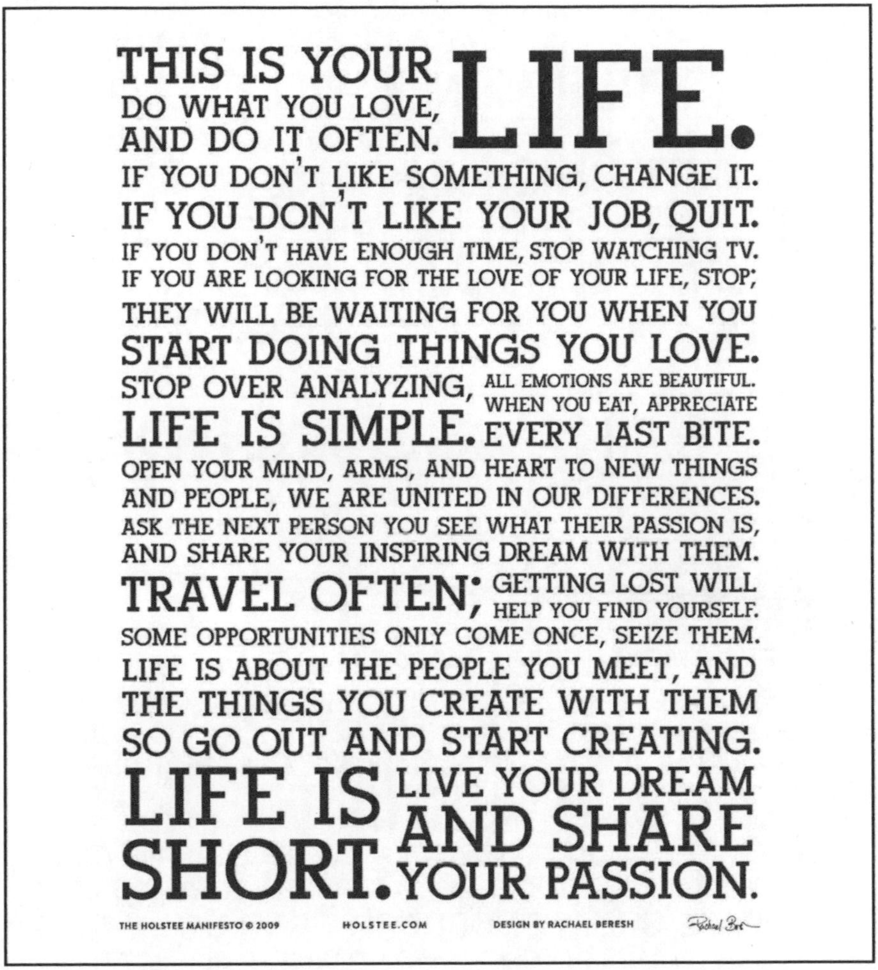

Source: © Holstee Inc. www.holstee.com.

I'm also a big advocate of the vision board (a collage of images of things you want in your life). My own is filled with lots of stuff I want to achieve and contribute to others, including book titles, travel destinations, health goals, a vision for the school and more. Who needs a business plan when you can have a vision board and a manifesto? Although business planning has its place, for most of us it has never ever been the determining factor of success.

Figure 4.2: my personal manifesto

LIVE WITH PURPOSE. DO WORK THAT I LOVE.
TRUST THAT MONEY WILL FOLLOW.
WRITE AND SPEAK FROM MY HEART.
BE AUTHENTIC. BE BRAVE. BE BOLD.
DON'T MIND SO MUCH WHAT OTHERS THINK.
SOFTEN MY HEART.
ASK EXCELLENT QUESTIONS.
REALLY LISTEN. NO, REALLY LISTEN.
SPEAK WISE WORDS.
BE KIND AND GENTLE ON OTHERS.
BE EVEN KINDER AND GENTLER ON MYSELF.
INSPIRE OTHERS.
HELP THEM BELIEVE ANYTHING IS POSSIBLE.
EXERCISE EVERY DAY. EAT HEALTHILY. LAUGH OFTEN.
JOURNAL, MEDITATE AND PRAY DAILY. READ A LOT. WATCH TED.
SMILE AT STRANGERS. MAKE SOMEONE'S DAY, EVERY DAY.
LOVE AND NURTURE MY SON.
REJOICE IN HIS GROWTH. LOVE AND SERVE MY CLIENTS.
DO GREAT THINGS FOR THEM. CELEBRATE OUR SUCCESSES.
CREATE GREAT PROSPERITY FOR US BOTH.
BE A LOVING FRIEND, SISTER AND DAUGHTER.
LISTEN. BE EMPATHETIC. JUST BE THERE. LISTEN. BE OPEN TO LOVE.
CREATE OPPORTUNITY. ATTRACT THE MAN I DESERVE.
EMBRACE COMMITMENT. TRAVEL FAR.
LIVE IN MANY COUNTRIES. COLLECT EXPERIENCES, NOT THINGS.
COLLABORATE. CONNECT. COOPERATE.
QUESTION EVERYTHING.
DREAM OF A BETTER WORLD.
DO SOMETHING ABOUT IT.

Creating a life of purpose and meaning requires a lot of internal soul searching. It takes time and sometimes it will be uncomfortable and confusing. The essential ingredients are a clear vision of what success means to you and a commitment to learning what you most need to learn to achieve that success. It's like a trek through the forest where there's no direct path to the other side. At times you'll stumble over boulders, at others you'll have to wade across creeks. You'll take some wrong turns and get lost and you'll have to hack down the long grass in front of you. Eventually you'll find your way to the other side and when you do, every experience you had in that forest will have added to your wisdom, your insight and your vision of the future.

Wondering what all this has to do with marketing? Everything! If you want to build a purpose-driven business that embraces conscious marketing principles, you'll need to understand deeply who you are, what you stand for, what success means to you and how you'll know when you get there.

A conscious business that practises conscious marketing cannot be built by an unconscious business leader. You have no choice but to keep doing the personal work to focus on your emotional, physical and spiritual wellbeing through continuous learning. Keep reading! The path to purpose is coming up!

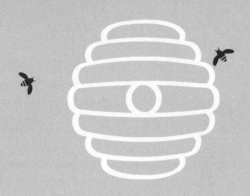

Chapter 5
Purpose (why)—the thing that keeps you keeping on

Roy Spence, author of *It's Not What You Sell, It's What You Stand For*, gave one of the most rousing presentations at a Conscious Capitalism conference I have encountered. In it he made this statement, which deeply affected me: 'The goal of our lives is to play to our strengths for the purpose of serving the greater good.'

We're entering an age where millions of people are seeking to lead a more enlightened and purpose-driven life, to serve others. We're turning inward and asking ourselves the deep questions. What is the purpose of my life? Why have I been put on this earth? What is the legacy I want to leave in this world?

Psychotherapist Victor Frankl's memoir *Man's Search for Meaning* chronicles his experiences in a German concentration camp and how he survived it. In the book he proposes a form of analysis he calls *logotherapy*. Unlike psychoanalysis, which tends to focus on the past, logotherapy (perhaps oversimplified here) confronts the patient with and reorients them towards the meaning of their life. *Logos* is a Greek word denoting 'word' or 'meaning'. Frankl argues that our search for meaning is our primary motivation in life, not a secondary rationalisation of instinctual drives. This meaning is unique and specific and can only be fulfilled by the person alone.

In a survey conducted by Johns Hopkins University that examined 7948 students from 48 colleges, students were asked what they considered most important to them. For 16 per cent of students it was 'making lots of money', while 78 per cent said their first goal was 'finding a purpose and meaning in my life'.

What if meaning and purpose were our new measure of success? What if meaning was the new money? What if we eliminated the boundaries between life and work and we all did work that fulfilled our life purpose? Is there even a difference between 'life purpose' and 'work purpose'?

As this is a business book, I focus here very much on business purpose rather than life or personal purpose, but for me they are indivisible in reality. Because I know my purpose in life and business, I just have work to do, but it doesn't ever feel like work.

When I gave up my old marketing business in 2010 and went to France for an extended period, I had no idea where my life and work would take me. While I was in France, my purpose was simple: to recover my mental, physical, creative and spiritual wellbeing. When I returned to Melbourne after that blissful experience, I found myself again purposeless, specifically in terms of how I was going to make a livelihood for the rest of my life. It was a mighty uncomfortable and stressful time. For almost three years my days and weeks were crammed with a range of activities that seemed to be in no way connected. I worked for a women's not-for-profit, did some consulting, ran business programs, started the Conscious Capitalism movement in Victoria, became actively involved in The Hub, travelled widely, blogged madly, published my memoir *Unstuck in Provence*, attended an endless number of events...and much more.

I had no idea then that each of these seemingly random activities had a purpose and that collectively they'd lead me to my new work purpose. I couldn't see how they were each interconnected and that they were leading me towards the reinvention of my livelihood, the birth of Slow School and the book you are now holding in your hands.

I feel so blessed that I found the courage to take the purpose journey. While I've paid a financial cost, it's also been the most valuable investment I've ever made in myself, my future, my son and the people I'm passionate about helping.

So if you're grappling with this notion of purpose, I encourage you wholeheartedly to make a commitment to the journey. I realise that for many, financial and family imperatives might persuade you that it's impossible. From firsthand experience, however, I can tell you that I've known many brave souls with not a dollar to their name who have nonetheless fearlessly pursued their personal path to purpose.

And please note, you do not need to run away from home to find your purpose. You can start where you are, right now, with what you have. My question to you is this: How much do you want it? If you want it badly enough you'll go there. One thing is for sure: action precedes clarity, every time, and yes, it will get messy!

Ready?

What is purpose anyway?

American author Robert Byrne says 'The purpose of life is a life of purpose'. But what is purpose? What does it really mean? Is it just another word for passion?

Of course there are many texts on the concept of purpose and as many definitions.

My definition:

Purpose is about living and working at the intersection of your talents, passions and strengths in service of the greater good. It's about having a life with a goal to do good and leave the world a better place because you existed.

Jim Carrey summed it up well in his commencement address at the Maharishi University of Management in 2014. Speaking to a large room filled with graduates, he urges them not choose their path out of fear and practicality but to ask the universe for what they truly want. He shares the story of his father who could have been a great comedian, but who just didn't believe it was possible. Instead he'd made a conservative decision to opt for a safe job as an accountant. He goes on to explain that after 12 years, his father was let go from that supposedly safe job and that the family had to do whatever it took to survive. He ends this story with a poignant statement '*I learnt many great lessons from my father, not the least of which was that you can fail at what you don't want, so you might as well take a chance at doing what you love.*'

Purpose is all about taking a chance at doing what you really love. What do you love? No, what do you *truly* love? As a parent, I want nothing more than to see my son create a vocation out of his passions. That's why I believe it's vital to ask our kids a different question—not the standard one about what they want to be when they grow up, but what they love to do right now, and then to help them create a business or a vocation from that. As adults, while we're asking our kids this question, surely we must be asking it of ourselves too?

Why purpose is the glue

Many of us reach a crossroads in life regarding our work, career or business. Often this can be as the result of a deeper, personal spiritual journey. It feels like we've outgrown our work. We start to question its value and if it's really making any difference. At this crossroads we consider the options—to get another job, start a new business or reinvent the business we have or, sadly, to do nothing and put up with it.

If we're not mindful or conscious, we risk jumping into something else too quickly or accepting an offer because it helps us avoid the pain we're currently in or because it makes us feel good (even if temporarily), or we simply need the money. And yes, I've definitely done this myself in the past, particularly in taking on clients with products and services I didn't believe in.

A clear purpose is like an anchor. It brings you back to your core, to your heart (not your head). It helps you make wise and mindful choices. It keeps you motivated to continue your life's work, even when the going gets tough. It helps you say no to the wrong kind of work (even if the money would be very helpful). It helps you attract the best circumstances, the best resources and the best people. Purpose, acted on diligently by a conscious leader, also generates prosperity, not just for you but for all you touch.

A well-articulated purpose has the power to ignite a nation, right the wrongs of the past and effect massive positive change. If you want to truly understand the power of purpose, listen to Martin Luther King Jr's spine-chilling 'I have a dream' speech from 1963. It was purpose that drove J.K. Rowling to keep on keeping on with her Harry Potter books after more than 30 knockbacks from publishing houses. It was purpose that drove Alexander Graham Bell (widely known as the inventor of the telephone) in his determination to invent a device that would help hearing-impaired people.

> Purpose, acted on diligently by a conscious leader, also generates prosperity, not just for you but for all you touch.

None of these individuals was driven by money or power. Rather, they were driven by a deep internal purpose to use their talents for the greater good. They were driven by meaning and the commitment to serve. As Pablo Picasso so succinctly put it, 'The meaning of life is to find your gift. The purpose of life is to give it away'. And that is his very gift to you.

Is purpose the new black?

Over the past few years, there's been a deluge of online tools, articles, books, courses, coaching programs and even whole businesses devoted to helping people find meaning and purpose. I love that they're collectively confirming the imperative of purpose and encouraging people to go on the journey.

> Purpose is *not* the new black. It's the imperative that will heal our world. It's serious work that must be tackled in a playful but wholehearted manner.

What I don't love is the number of businesspeople who are treating 'purpose' as the new black, as a slick marketing message to hook in new customers. If you encounter companies waxing lyrical about purpose while practising unconscious marketing and hard-sell sales techniques, keep searching.

Many qualified, reputable professionals provide the deep, long-term support you will need when doing the inner work necessary to help you tap your purpose. If you're serious about it, know that your success will most likely depend on a combination of your own efforts and the support of a qualified mentor or counsellor.

Purpose is *not* the new black. It's the imperative that will heal our world. It's serious work that must be tackled in a playful but wholehearted manner. If you want a life of purpose, be careful what you wish for, because you just might get it!

Vision and purpose—what's the difference?

Now let's move into the realm of purpose for business. Is a purpose different from a vision? If so, how? There seem to be so many definitions around these ideas, so I've simplified them here in my own words:

- *Purpose* (why): a statement of why your company exists and how your business makes a difference (sometimes referred to as a mission)

- *Vision* (what): a statement of what the world will look like when your purpose is realised.

A great role model and proof that there is a 'purpose for purpose' is the Interface story.

Interface, Inc.: the story of a 'reformed plunderer'

In 1973, Ray Anderson (who died in 2011) founded a carpet company, which he built up into the Interface success story through servicing the business and corporate world in the US and globally. In the summer of 1994 Ray experienced an awakening after reading Paul Hawken's book *The Ecology of Commerce*. This book charges business and industry with the destruction of the biosphere and argues that the 'take, make and waste' industrial model is simply unsustainable. In Ray's famous TED talk of 2009, he refers to himself as a reformed plunderer, declaring that his own company (a petroleum-intensive enterprise) and those of his peers should be considered criminals who have stolen our children's future. Ray's epiphany revolutionised Interface's business strategy from that day forward and today the company is a global leader in sustainable business. Its mission (purpose) is to be the first company to become fully sustainable with zero negative impact by 2020.

Because of this transformation, Interface is increasingly prosperous, growing exponentially and outperforming the competition. Interface has proven that you can be purpose-driven and wildly profitable.

Imagine the alternative. What if Ray had not read that book? What if he'd gone on with business as usual, like so many of his peers? Would the company even still be in business? And what of his competition? I wonder how they have responded to Ray's industry leadership?

The pursuit of a common purpose that is, at its core, about doing no harm and serving the greater good just might be our greatest leveller and the path to healing capitalism and the planet.

How to find your purpose

Where do I start on this one? My first piece of advice is just get started, and keep Martin Luther King Jr's words in mind: 'Faith is taking the first step even when you don't see the whole staircase'.

If you've spent many years doing work you don't love for people you don't love and haven't thought about this notion of having a purpose-driven vocation, you'll need to be gentle on yourself. The model in figure 5.1 is a good place to start. Allocate time to thinking, meditating on, exploring and writing about each of the circles.

Figure 5.1: the Discover your Purpose model

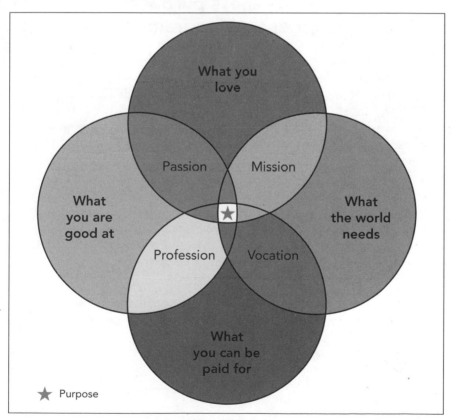

If you already have a business, this model is still very useful if you are looking to affirm you're on track, to refresh your business or even to reinvent it from the ground up. At the intersection of these circles you will find your purpose.

You've no doubt spent years acquiring skills, talents, qualifications, experience and knowledge and building your networks and contacts. And during this time you've developed a healthy array of beliefs, values and issues you're passionate about. The most useful place to start, then, is to review your past and the periods in your life when you felt most alive and were doing things you loved. While it might be tempting to wipe the slate clean and start over, your history is often the very solid platform on which to base a new purpose and to rebuild your business.

Monique goes deep to find her business purpose (The Customer Service Training Group)

One of my students, Monique, is a brilliant and sought-after expert in customer service training who runs her own company and works with many large corporations. Having been doing this for more than 12 years, she is highly regarded and has made a healthy income from her work. Despite this, she found herself experiencing a growing dissatisfaction with her work and business. She was disenchanted that many of the people attending her training workshops were unable to offer greater service because of inherent system problems, a lack of service culture and poor leadership. She was disillusioned by the lack of opportunity provided to leaders to support their team and provide a strong service culture. Finally, she was questioning whether her training (as brilliant as it was) could ever have a long-term positive impact on the people, the organisation and ultimately the customer, without leadership support.

So let me demonstrate how Monique used the purpose model (figure 5.1, p. 75) to arrive at her very clear purpose statement.

What you love

These are the issues you are passionate about, the things you want to change or to fix—your mission.

Monique is passionate about customer service. She believes that brilliant customer service can obviate the need for expensive marketing. She is passionate about inspiring and engaging leaders at all levels on how vital customer service is to the future of the organisation and how they can create a great service culture. She is passionate about showing the business world at large that the barriers to an employee providing brilliant service go way beyond lack of care. (In her cause-leading white paper, she gives an example of company management that expects brilliant customer service from their call centre staff but don't have the systems in place to enable great service.) She is passionate about working deeply with organisations on their service culture rather than just delivering a few training courses. She wants to challenge the customer service education and training status quo by bringing innovative learning techniques and practices to her work. She believes that brilliant customer service has the power to change people's daily lives. In short, Monique is passionate about changing both the service culture and the education and training programs required to effect deep and lasting change. <u>What are you passionate about changing?</u>

<u>What you are good at</u>

These are your strengths—the skills you bring to the table.

Monique is skilled at establishing and building lasting relationships, facilitating and questioning, motivating individuals, creating awesome content and courses, and integrating her work in organisations with ongoing support tools and mentoring. Equally, like all of us, there are some things she is not so good at. It's handy while focusing on this circle to identify these areas so you can find the right resources/people to help. Spending time on becoming average at what you are not good at makes little sense. What are you good at? What do you want to become even better at?

What the world needs

How can your talents and skills make a difference?

Monique believes that people must demonstrate more genuine care for each other. She believes that by revolutionising customer service culture, particularly in Australia (where it is sorely lacking), people everywhere can make a big difference to those they serve. She believes that to create a healthy, vibrant service culture everyone in an organisation must be engaged. What does the world need that you can offer?

(continued)

Monique goes deep to find her business purpose (cont'd)

What you can be paid for

How do you make a livelihood from your calling?

Monique is repositioning her business to align with the other three circles (figure 5.1, p. 75) and is rebuilding her training programs in accordance with her beliefs and vision for a better service culture in organisations. She is considering deeply the kinds of clients she wants to work with—those who share her values. She is packaging her services so that she can work directly with a niche number of organisations at all levels and on a bigger scale for the longer term. She is making a difference, one organisation, one employee and one customer at a time. What can you create that makes a real difference and that you can be remunerated well for?

After all this, what is Monique's purpose?

Monique is still in the very early stages of fulfilling her purpose by developing her business in this new direction. Backed by her paper (e-book) she is now slowly and steadily, week by week, starting to have deeper and more meaningful conversations about her purpose and mission to change the service culture in Australia.

As a result of doing this deep work, Monique is now publicly and happily declaring her new business purpose: To transform customer service culture through leadership and learning.

Digging deep on purpose

In addition to the circles in figure 5.1 (p. 75) and the example of Monique, I thoroughly recommend you take time out to consider the following questions. Start a 'purpose' journal and write down your answers to the questions, addressing perhaps one question a day. Build on this purpose questioning by dipping into other resources—talks, papers, books, videos—to supplement your thinking. A commitment to 30 minutes a day with some deep mindfulness practices will help you on your way. Then find a 'purpose buddy', a qualified adviser/counsellor/mentor, or join a community such as Slow School to discuss and share your work.

The objective of tackling the foregoing exercise and the questions that follow is to help you to develop a purpose statement of, say, five to 15 words that clearly articulates your big *why*.

My own path to purpose was pretty haphazard and involved myriad ideas, people, communities and resources to help me get there. I hope this book will help you achieve your goal less haphazardly than I did!

Now grab your journal and ponder these questions:

1 Am I content with where my life is heading?

2 What would I like to change?

3 If I could do anything in the world what would it be?

4 What do I have the most fun doing?

5 What makes me lose all track of time?

6 What makes me feel happy and fulfilled?

7 What does success look like to me?

8 What abilities and talents have I been blessed with?

9 What do people most often compliment me for?

10 What do people most often ask me for help with?

11 What talents would I continue to use even if I wasn't being paid?

12 What activities have I participated in that have brought me most joy? Why?

13 What have been my most enjoyable jobs? Why?

14 What challenges have I had to overcome? What have I learned from them?

15 What lessons have I learned in my life?

16 What insights have I gained from them?

17 What changes or new ideas could I bring into the world?

18 What is broken in the world that I really want to fix?

19 Why would I want to fix it? How would I fix it?

20 Why is it that important to me?

21 Why is that important?

22 Why is that important?

23 Why is that important? Keep asking this question and record all the answers. Make sure your answers drill right down to your personal story (most whys come back to this).

This is also a great exercise to do in groups so others can give you feedback on what they observe.

Although your answers must come from within, having a good guide by your side to ask the questions and probe you further can be very helpful.

If you're in a business partnership or are a team member of a larger business, the questions can make for very meaningful dialogue. If you're contemplating a business partnership, this would be a great exercise for each of you to complete before you dive headlong into it. Too many business (and life) partnerships fail because of a lack of shared purpose or because of misaligned purpose and vision. Don't let this happen to you.

And now to your company purpose statement.

From your answers to the questions, review and highlight the words that stand out. List the most powerful words for you, then craft them into a purpose statement of five to 15 words, which can then be shortened to a one-line statement. Don't worry too much about the actual words; focus on the intent behind the words. Your initial goal is to tell it straight, not necessarily great. That will come once you truly *feel* your purpose—physically, mentally, emotionally and spiritually.

> Too many business (and life) partnerships fail because of a lack of shared purpose or because of misaligned purpose and vision. Don't let this happen to you.

Some great purpose statements

Following are URLs to some great purpose statements adopted by companies, both large and small, from all over the world. One of the best ways to get inspiration around purpose and build a purpose-driven business is to study the companies that have a great stated purpose that you can see is being integrated deeply into every tiny corner of the company.

- Accounting Solutions
  www.asl.co.nz/about_us/our-story

- American Red Cross
  www.redcross.org/about-us/mission

- Hitnet
  www.hitnet.com.au

- Hub Australia
  www.hubaustralia.com/about/impact

- Intrepid Travel
  www.intrepidtravel.com/about-intrepid

- Patagonia
  www.patagonia.com/us/patagonia.go?assetid=2047

- Red Balloon
  www.redballoon.com.au/about-us

- Seated Massage
  www.seatedmassage.com.au

- Southwest Airlines
  www.southwest.com/html/about-southwest/index.html

- Starbucks
  www.starbucks.com.au/Mission-Statement.php

- The Slow School of Business (Slow School)
  www.slowschool.com.au

- TOMS
  www.toms.com

- Whole Kids
  www.wholekids.com.au/whole-kids-about-us/our-reason-for-being

- Wood & Grieve Engineers
  www.wge.com.au/our-culture

How to know if you're 'on purpose'

Many of my clients and students spend months (even years) working on their purpose. When they do crack it, they find a voice they never thought they had. They talk with a conviction they've never articulated before around their purpose and how their business is effecting change. Most importantly it spurs them into action. Their work becomes an imperative, something they just have to do. As a mentor, it's the most wonderful feeling working with a client who discovers their true purpose and who starts to take bold actions to bring it to life, which ironically is exactly why I do what I do—there's literally no shutting them up!

Here are some questions to ask yourself that will help you determine if you have really found your purpose.

- Does it make you cry? Do you get tingles when you think about it?

- Do you get up every morning itching to get to work?

- Do you incessantly think about your business and how it will help others?

- Do you actually complete your 'to do' lists?

- Would you do what you're doing even if you weren't getting paid?

- Do you have an energy, vitality and enthusiasm you never had before?

- Do others remark on this? Do you inspire others to get stuck into their purpose?

- Are you attracting people, events or opportunities into your life in a way you never could before?

- Do people offer to help you even without being asked?

- Do people freely share what you are up to with others without being asked?

- Do you find it easy to engage others in your purpose conversation?

- Are you acquiring new contacts and clients without great effort?

- Are other people referring you, building your contacts, connections, clients or new business?

- Are you confident about taking action even if you're uncertain of the outcome?

- Do you feel empowered and able to make decisions without worrying about it?

- Do you have a feeling of trust and faith that it will all work out for the best?

- Do you feel no stress when there are bumps in the road?

When you find your purpose, you will know it in every cell of your body. I know this because I've been there and I'm now doing it, and so are many of our students. You will know it intuitively: as Albert Einstein affirmed, 'The only real valuable thing is intuition'.

> A money-driven purpose does not ensure the resilience you'll need when times get tough (and they will, as they do for us all). A purpose-driven business keeps you inspired to deliver, rain, hail or shine.

Recently, at one of our numerous Slow School dinners, I was talking with one of my students about the new business venture she was about to embark on. We were discussing her fears around it and where she was stuck. I asked her *why* she wanted to start the online business she had in mind. She wanted to make the most of her IT skills, be her own boss and enjoy flexible working arrangements. Finally, after many more prodding questions, she admitted that her ultimate motivation was to make money.

This will be the very reason the business will struggle, if it even gets off the ground. A money-driven purpose does not ensure the resilience you'll need when times get tough (and they will, as they do for us all). A purpose-driven business keeps you inspired to deliver, rain, hail or shine.

Money is just one motivator. It is not your purpose.

Why is purpose at the heart of conscious marketing?

Simon Sinek, in *Start with Why*, states, 'People don't buy what you do, they buy *why* you do it'. And that's why we need to have wholehearted conversations that shift from talking about products and services (the what) to purpose (the why).

Have you ever been at one of those painful networking events where everyone seems to be giving their rehearsed, cheesy elevator pitch? You know the one. 'I'm an accountant, but what I really do is help my clients pay the tax office less money.' Yawn.

In the push and shove of today's fast-paced world of business, we're being told it's vital to have a compelling elevator pitch. In mere seconds you're expected to excite someone by what you do, what you offer and how you transform your clients' lives. You're expected to be 'pitch perfect'. I used to teach this stuff many years ago, although I had a different term for it then. I called it the 'verbal brand'.

Now, many years later, I think it's a load of bull. Sure I'd like to know what you do (that you're an accountant, financial planner, graphic designer or whatever), but I'm far more interested in *why* you do what you do—your purpose for being in business, what really gets you fired up and how you're making a difference. And sadly, *why* can't be squeezed into a pithy and over-rehearsed elevator pitch. *Why* is communicated with passion, excitement and maybe even a swear word or two. The *why* is authentic, imperfect, unconstrained. It's full of stories and shocking statistics and other stuff the person never knew they needed to know.

Your *why* ignites a deep, earthy conversation. It connects you to others in a way that no elevator pitch will ever do. Most often you won't even need to state your purpose—it will come out in the course of the conversation. In a purpose conversation, as you share the deep stuff you move through the 'know, like, trust' steps fluidly. Or the conversation will stop dead in its tracks. That's how you'll know if you've found a person dedicated to purpose.

Old-school marketing is functional. It's about manufacturing emotion to manipulate people, jumping straight into showcasing products, highlighting features, promoting benefits and talking price. New-school marketing is never about manipulation. It's about engaging people with your raison d'être. That's why purpose is at the heart of a complete and conscious approach to marketing. Old mass marketing techniques no longer need be applied. The stories around purpose-driven companies spread like ripples in a pond.

> The stories around purpose-driven companies spread like ripples in a pond.

People buy you. They buy your cause. They buy what you believe in, what you stand for, your purpose. What do you believe in? What do you want to fix that's broken? This is at the heart of what conscious marketing is all about.

Purpose is the piece that is set in stone. It's the glue that ensures your business flourishes. It's also the point from which you develop the bigger vision for your company. Purpose (the why) and vision (the what) go hand in hand with your values (what you stand for). Together they motivate you to keep on keeping on.

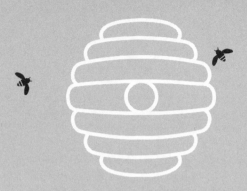

Chapter 6
Product (what)—those things you offer that improve lives

Your products and services are the manifestation of your purpose. They bring your purpose and vision to life. Every product you offer, every service you deliver, every customer experience you provide, reflects whether your business is fulfilling its purpose.

Your aim is to build products and services that are so good and so compelling that people simply want to buy, stick with you and spread the word.

In our fast-to-market, fast-money world we are easily diverted from our real purpose, which is ultimately to serve a need and improve lives. The companies that spend more time truly understanding this as they build their products will gain the most attention and attract the people that matter and care.

Great companies are not built on great products, they are built on great people—people who share the purpose and are intrinsically motivated to serve others with great products. (I was tempted actually to put People before Product in this model, but as each element depends on each of the others, I decided to leave it as is.)

Conscious business leaders and owners continuously learn about and utilise the newest and cleverest adaptive business tools and models to build truly compelling products and services. These new business-planning models supersede the out-dated and conventional business plans of old. They put purpose at the core, they are flexible and robust, and they consider every stakeholder in the production and delivery of products, not just the customer.

A useful tool to get you started

A great book to help you define your product or service offering and how it will be resourced and distributed is Osterwalder and Pigneur's *Business Model Generation*. This handbook is for visionaries, game changers and challengers who are willing to defy outmoded business models to design tomorrow's enterprises.

The Business Model Canvas (see figure 6.1) is a one-page tool that offers a shared language for describing, visualising, assessing and changing business models. It's based on nine basic building blocks that show the logic of how a company intends to become financially viable.

Figure 6.1: the Business Model Canvas

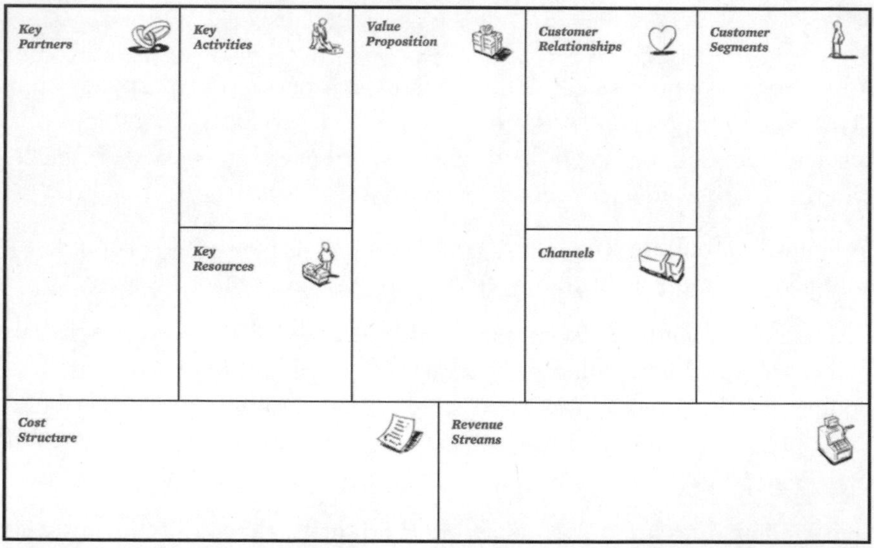

Source: © Osterwalder, A. 2009. *Business Model Generation: A Handbook for Visionaries, Game Changers, and Challengers*. John Wiley and Sons Inc.

The first two building blocks are at the core of our third element, Product, or what it is that we are offering the market—the first block is the 'customer segment', the second the 'value proposition'. Together they describe the bundle of products and services that will be created for a specific customer segment. In these building blocks, we ask ourselves what value we deliver to the customer, what problems we solve, what needs we satisfy, and what bundles of products or services we offer that fill these needs.

I recommend taking a look at this tool to gain an overall picture of your business model as you consider the products or services you develop and then deliver them to the market.

Now let's look at some of the fundamentals you need to consider in building your product or service offering. What is the product? Who does it serve? Why do they need it? How much will they pay? How will they get it? How does it fit with your purpose?

The products and services you offer

Wealth, like happiness, is never attained when sought after directly. It comes as a by-product of providing a useful service.

Henry Ford

If you've spent considerable time working on your personal development and refining your purpose and why you exist, you'll find your current suite of products or services no longer serve you or your clients. They'll need an overhaul.

Conversely, you may notice that your products or services are no longer meeting needs, that you're losing clients or that your service has become commoditised and price-sensitive. These are real signs that you'll need to turn inward and do the purpose work first before reinventing your offering. It truly doesn't matter what existential events occur to set you on the path to purpose for your business. However it happens, it's a gift!

If you're in a business that's been around for a long time and is pretty tired, I thoroughly recommend using the Business Model Canvas and imagining your business as a start-up again. Work with a mindset that the old business will become insolvent while the new business emerges into the new economy.

> It truly doesn't matter what existential events occur to set you on the path to purpose for your business. However it happens, it's a gift!

I've long been disenchanted with the accounting industry. As one of more than a million very small business owners in Australia, I believe that we're truly underserved and undervalued by this industry. After more than 10 years in business, three different bookkeepers and three different accountants, I'd all but given up on the idea of finance and accounting ever being simple, manageable and pleasurable. Like many small business owners, having my eyeteeth pulled without an anaesthetic was a more appealing prospect than doing my financials and working with my accountant. I desperately wanted an accountant who would actually care about me and my business, would be willing to educate me and not use jargon or technical language to keep me reliant on them, and would make it all simple while not using time-based billing.

In 2013, I came across Nudge Accounting.

Nudge Accounting: a service offering that stands out from the crowd

Emma Petroulas is one of the three founding partners of this national accounting firm that started up just two years ago. As an ex-corporate accountant who (like her partners) grew up in a family business, Emma has a deep empathy for small business owners and a real purpose and passion to serve them. Nudge's service offering is so very different from those of most other accounting firms. They've dared to be different by shaking up a tired industry in every conceivable way.

So how are they different? In addition to truly caring and sharing their wisdom, they combine the bookkeeping, accounting and tax services under one roof, using the smartest accounting platforms such as Xero and other technology platforms such as Box (a free cloud storage system that allows you to photograph and store receipts and upload documents). They do not use time-based billing. For one reasonable monthly fee charged to your credit card (they have three service and price offerings depending on your number of transactions) you get a seamless, integrated accounting service that includes bookkeeping, monthly reporting, BAS calculations and annual tax returns. I've now been with them for more than 12 months and I can't recommend them highly enough. And the best part? After all these years I love doing my accounts and taking control of my finances, and they now get done on a timely basis every single month.

Nudge threw every conventional accounting practice out the window. They addressed what was broken in a tired industry and developed a business with purpose and soul and a complete service offering that stands out from the crowd. They've truly understood that their role is to serve a desperate need in the small business market. Because of this, they've not had to undertake any conventional marketing or paid advertising. Their business has grown through word-of-mouth and through clients like me sharing the love! They're true practitioners of conscious marketing.

What can you do to take a page out of Nudge's book?

How do you know if people want it?

In developing their disruptive business model and service offering, Nudge didn't just build a product and throw it out to the market in the hope it would stick. They did some serious homework first. They asked many small business owners what they didn't like about their accountant — such as charging in six-minute increments, unsubstantiated billing, uncertainty around their financial performance and being treated as a low-priority client behind higher fee paying clients.

They also searched exhaustively for (and tested) the best technology platform on which to build their service offering (accounting and cloud storage), then they built a prototype model and piloted it for many months with target market clients for free. They listened attentively to what clients told them — what they liked, what they didn't and how the service offering could truly serve every need.

They adopted what is commonly known as a 'minimum viable product' offering until such time that they knew the service would stack up and they'd done the financial projections.

We also adopted a 'minimum viable product' approach at Slow School. In 2014, over five months, we hosted around 25 classes and events that were attended by almost 500 people. At these classes I shared the purpose, vision and values of the school while asking people for feedback at every opportunity. We used free technology platforms to let people know about the school — WordPress (for the website as a sub-page on my Carolyn Tate & Co. website), Eventbrite (to publish and market events), MailChimp (for mailing to our database) and Twitter, Facebook and LinkedIn (for social media sharing). I also asked for (and was offered) help from people who shared the purpose and vision and who had brilliant skills to contribute—facilitators, a videographer, a copywriter, a researcher, a designer, advisers, a project manager and more. And I asked The Hub to be our community partner and provide the classroom for free while we were testing the viability.

While we gathered interest and listened, I worked with two trusted and experienced advisers on the business model. And we undertook three research projects, one with participants in our beta test classes, one with the volunteer team and one larger piece with the attendees of the classes themselves. During this whole time we tested the school's viability without spending any money (and have even made a bit) in order to prove that Slow School is a desirable education option for business owners. Only now in 2015 will we invest in the infrastructure required to bring it to life on a bigger scale.

If you're despondent about the lack of interest in, and subsequent sales of, your products or services, it's most likely that you've missed this vital step. I talk with so many people who have wasted valuable resources (money and time) on employing people, building products, branding, websites and countless other things only to find that *no one wants to buy*. It's heartbreaking.

In today's cluttered and noisy marketplace, if you don't actually spend the time testing and listening (repeatedly) it will be nigh on impossible to build a product or service that fills a need, unless of course you have megabucks and can use manipulative mass-marketing tactics to create false needs. Far better to do it quietly, consistently and gently and build something brilliant that people need and that will sell itself. What will you do to test and retest?

Who do you serve?

Many years ago I was running a marketing workshop with financial planners from a major Australian funds management company. We were discussing target markets and ideal clients. Most of the planners declared that their ideal clients were high-net-worth individuals, until one smart chap piped up, 'The truth is we'll all take anyone that's breathing', which caused a ripple of laughter around the room. They went on to talk about the functional and rational attributes of their target market—gender, income, profession, marital status, number of properties owned, where they lived, education, number of kids and so on. What struck me was how coldly impersonal the whole conversation was. There was a distinct absence of feeling and emotion in the room and no discussion around the real needs, worries and aspirations of their clients.

A company that takes an 'anyone will do' approach or that focuses purely on the functional and rational attributes of their target market is destined for failure. On the other hand, the company that focuses on the internal stuff, the emotional and spiritual needs of the customer, will be impossible to emulate.

In our technology-driven world it's now possible to deliver offerings to niche groups that share a common interest, passion, values, problems, goals or desires. We are now called to think of our potential customers in terms of the unquantifiable and unmeasurable aspects of their lives. In the new world economy these people simply don't fit into neat little demographic bundles.

And as we become increasingly conscious of whom we're buying from and of the impact our purchases will have on people and the planet, we'll choose to buy from companies that

> The company that focuses on the internal stuff, the emotional and spiritual needs of the customer, will be impossible to emulate.

share our values and ethics, that have a purpose beyond making a profit and that offer disruptive products and services to match our needs.

Who do you serve? How much do you really know about what they need? How do you know if they share your *why*?

So what do they need?

Nudge Accounting were very clear that they were called to serve the small business owners who felt disenfranchised and underserved by the accounting industry. They put themselves in their clients' shoes, felt their pain and worked with empathy throughout the whole process of developing their business and their service offering.

Going beyond demographic characteristics to understand the concerns, behaviours and aspirations of your ideal client is the secret ingredient to conscious marketing. In the book *Business Model Generation* there's a brilliant 'Empathy Map' to help you truly understand your ideal clients' beliefs, values and motivations. The map helps you identify what they think and feel, what they see and do, where their pain is, and what they might hope to gain from buying your product or service. It's a great tool to help you dig deep and find out what's really going on and how your product can help.

Are your clients just a number to you or do you have true empathy for them? What can you do to get better acquainted with their very real needs?

The price you pay

As we emerge from the industrial age into the enlightened technology age, we find ourselves increasingly confused about how to price our products and services. On the one hand, we live in a price-war culture (think about the price-driven car, homewares and clothing industries); on the other hand, we live in a free culture (think Google, Wikipedia, Facebook, eBay, online learning, and music and movie downloads).

When it comes to professional services such as consulting, accounting and law, where we've traditionally charged for our time, pricing models are also becoming increasingly disrupted. Nothing is as it used to be.

If you find yourself being beaten down on price and always having to pitch for work, chances are you're going to have to make some serious changes. And while it's tempting to look sideways to the competition as a benchmark for your pricing model, it's most likely going to be a very unhelpful place to start.

It's likely that you'll have to go back to purpose to reinvent your service offering from the ground up, along with your pricing models and options.

If you happen to be one of the thousands of independent professionals (solo business operators who sell time for dollars) in Australia, you'll know how competitive the marketplace is and how often price is the driver of whether clients buy or not. You'll be very keen to understand how to move from selling time to selling 'value' and how to communicate that effectively to potential clients.

So how do you sell your value rather your time? There's a great little fable called 'Breaking the Time Barrier' written by Mike McDerment, co-founder and CEO of FreshBooks. It's the story of Steve, a web developer who is consistently undercharging for his services based on time versus value. Steve reaches out to Karen, who has built a very healthy business offering a similar service to Steve's, based on selling value and outcomes versus time. In summary, the fable highlights the importance of being able to probe and ask the right questions of clients and to have deep and meaningful conversations about their true needs, problems and aspirations *before* having any cost or price discussion.

The deeper you understand your clients and how you can make a difference to their business, the more trust is engendered, the more value you can offer and the more money you can ask for.

Trust is the essential ingredient of being able to charge on value versus hours. So what questions might work for you in engendering trust? What problem am I really solving for the client? What type of value does my service offering create? What unique insights, experience, resources or connections can I offer to clients?

> Trust is the essential ingredient of being able to charge on value versus hours.

What would it cost the client *not* to solve the problem they have? Is the value of the outcome greater than the cost of what you are fixing for them?

Yet there's an opportunity to go even deeper than this. Conscious companies dedicated to making a positive impact in the world are increasingly choosing to partner with companies that have a shared purpose and values. If your business relationship remains at a one-dimensional level, with 'value' being measured merely in financial or rational terms, then you'll eventually find yourself competing again. When customers buy the *why* (your purpose) behind what you do, not just what you offer, true trust is engendered and real value is exchanged, for the long term.

No matter what you're selling, the best way to ensure that you give and receive the value you deserve for your efforts is to start with a shared purpose. What real value do you create for your customers?

From demand to delivery

Whenever you find yourself on the side of the majority,
it is time to pause and reflect.

Mark Twain

No matter how widely accessible your product or service is, if there's no demand, there's no sale. Conscious business leaders take a truly different approach to distribution and delivery. They start small and create demand in their niche markets before opening up channels of distribution more broadly.

They ask good questions of the early adopters and they listen carefully to the responses. They use these insights and their own intuition to make incremental improvements and to keep people engaged and involved. They create an underground movement and grow their entity from the nucleus of their tribe.

KeepCup: a timely assault on our throwaway culture

Many years ago, Melbourne café owner Abigail Forsyth found herself drinking coffee from disposable cups like billions of other takeaway coffee drinkers around the world. She was unhappy about the consequences of the disposable coffee-cup culture (over 500 billion disposable cups are manufactured every year, or about 75 disposable cups for every single person on the planet) so with her brother she decided to do something about it. In 2009 they launched the KeepCup, a reusable coffee cup made locally of plastics or glass.

The company has a mission to eliminate the use of disposable plastics by encouraging people to use reusable cups. They're now delivering a global campaign that aims to kick-start the demise of the disposable and change the way people think about the convenience culture. (Over a year, the use of a KeepCup reduces greenhouse gas emissions by up to 92 per cent compared with disposable coffee cups.)

While they started small, they soon found demand growing and distribution channels expanding as a result. Now, some five years later, they've sold more than 3 million KeepCups through 271 retailers in Australia and in 32 other countries around the world. They also sell customised cups online. KeepCup have earned certification as a B Corporation, joining over a thousand B Corporations globally—all companies meeting rigorous standards that measure a company's impact on its employees, suppliers and community and the environment.

KeepCup have built a growing movement around their purpose, and a growing demand for their product as a result. I've used my own bright pink KeepCup for around two years now. I take it with me in my handbag everywhere, just as I do my wallet and keys. Each time I use it I'm reminded of the small contribution I'm making in the world, and encourage others to make a small investment for a big impact.

KeepCup are true practitioners of conscious marketing. They spend little (if any) money on traditional marketing or advertising because they've created a movement around their brand to attract the people who really care and who are more than willing to spread the word. What can your business learn from the KeepCup story?

The customer experience

When companies are driven by profit and offer undifferentiated services, such as those in much of the telecommunications and banking industries, customers tend to have very little tolerance for poor service or substandard delivery. They also have very little loyalty.

On the other hand, purpose-driven companies passionate about change, with conscious, caring leaders and a conscious, open culture will often be forgiven if something doesn't meet the customer's service expectations. Such is the power of purpose.

Conscious marketing is all about building something so fundamentally good and compelling right into the heart of your business and your products and services that everyone (suppliers, employees, community and so on) wants to join your tribe and spread the word.

And that of course encompasses the customer service experience—how you interact and deal with the customer from the first point of contact until long after the sale.

> When companies are driven by profit and offer undifferentiated services...customers tend to have very little tolerance for poor service or substandard delivery. They also have very little loyalty.

Zappos: 'powered by service'

There's no company quite like Zappos when it comes to customer service. Zappos is an online retailer based in Las Vegas that sells shoes and clothing. Their tagline is 'powered by service' and they have aligned their whole company around their purpose—to provide the best customer service possible. Their aim is to exceed the customer's expectations every time, through an array of service standards such as free shipping and return and even up to 365 days for a customer to return their products without question. They also warehouse all stock for sale and only advertise stock on hand, so they can guarantee timely delivery.

Tony Hsieh, founder of Zappos and author of *Delivering Happiness*, has said: 'We asked ourselves what we wanted this company to stand for. We didn't want to just sell shoes. I wasn't even into shoes—but I was passionate about customer service.'

Their culture is their biggest asset and they're a Fortune 100 best company to work for. Their core values encourage delivering great service, open-mindedness, doing more with less, humility, positivity and being passionate, just to name a few.

Zappo's public reputation as a leader in customer service and culture has attracted thousands of businesspeople eager to understand just how they've done it. So instead of keeping their secrets to themselves, they've built Zappos Insights, a business school aimed at educating business leaders on how to replicate the Zappos service culture. Each month they receive 1500 visitors on their campus in downtown Las Vegas, while they also run quarterly three-day culture camps and offer membership to their online education program.

Zappos are real practitioners of conscious marketing. They understand that having a higher purpose, brilliant products and outstanding customer service is all the marketing required to attract the brightest staff and the most loyal customers. If you haven't done so already, they're definitely worth investigating!

We've covered a lot in this chapter on what you offer to the market that brings your purpose to life. If you're wondering where to start, I recommend spending a few hours reading around the case studies (there's nothing so inspiring as studying those who are doing it well already), accessing the Business Model Canvas (figure 6.1, p. 88) and journaling about the questions posed.

There's a long list of inspirational Certified B Corporations you can research too; visit www.bcorporation.net.

In summary...

> Personal consciousness + Higher purpose + Game-changing products and services + Outstanding customer service = Conscious marketing.

Companies that focus on these areas, working from the inside out, will attract the best people, opportunities and circumstances needed to flourish, and this means there'll be very little need for conventional paid mass-marketing and advertising. Hooray!

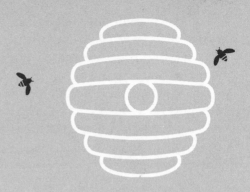

Chapter 7

People and planet (who)—the partners in your business community

When we try to pick out anything by itself, we find it hitched to everything else in the universe.

John Muir

In the previous chapter we focused predominantly on the product you're delivering to your customers, the people who invest in your services. Here we turn to the collective power to be derived from nurturing all stakeholders integral to your business community: your employees and suppliers, investors, the industry you operate in, your competitors, your friends and family, the local community and of course the planet.

So many companies neglect to nurture *all* stakeholders in their ecosystem. Too often their attention is focused single-mindedly on customers (who fill the till) and shareholders or business owners (who empty it). Most stakeholders are plundered to meet the profit demands of companies, and the number one victim is usually the environment.

Conscious business leaders understand that a sustainable business is built on purpose and people (and the planet) before products and profit. They gather their tribe from across their stakeholder groups by sharing their purpose and vision and actively walking the talk when it comes to their values. They take a humble, servant-leadership approach and put themselves in the shoes of every person they rely on to help them deliver their services to the market. They engage with the partners required to help them build products and services so they are their proudest advocates.

> Conscious business leaders understand that a sustainable business is built on purpose and people (and the planet) before products and profit.

In this chapter we discuss each of these stakeholder groups (or partners) and look at some examples of companies that are working with them in mutually beneficial and meaningful ways for the prosperity of all.

The planet and the environment

Of course the ultimate stakeholder is the planet and the environment. Thankfully, companies are now overwhelmingly starting to recognise that if they don't seriously address the 'take, make and waste' practices that Ray Anderson of Interface identified, they'll find themselves without a future.

The B Impact Assessment is a wonderful place to start to understand your environmental footprint and how you might reduce it or even contribute positively to the regeneration of the environment. The B Impact Assessment tool gives you a baseline rating on how your company performs against dozens of best practices on employee, community and environmental impact. It takes just 90 minutes to complete. When you've finished you can compare yourself to some of the world's best companies and receive customised improvement reports. It's truly an eye-opening exercise for any business leader.

There's much to be gained from studying communities and even whole countries that are adopting serious sustainable environmental practices. One such country is Sweden.

Sweden: a trailblazer in sustainable development

For most Swedes today, sustainability is a way of life. With a population of 9.7 million, Sweden ranks first in the EU in production of organic foods, leads the way in recycling drink cans and bottles, and derives the highest share of its energy from renewable sources.

The core principle behind sustainable development is acting to conserve resources for future generations. In 1975, Sweden recycled 38 per cent of household waste. Today, incredibly, less than 1 per cent of household waste ends up as landfill, with 99 per cent recycled in one way or another. Most Swedes separate their recycling at home before taking it to local recycling stations, which are located within 300 metres of every residential area. Household waste is burned at one of 32 incineration plants that provide heat for 810 000 households and electricity for 250 000 private homes.

Renewable resources provide 48 per cent of Sweden's energy needs, compared with 13 per cent in Australia. In Europe, where the organic food market is growing 5 to 7 per cent annually, Sweden ranks at the top of the green shoppers list.

Despite a crippling period in the 1990s when the country was hit by a serious financial crisis that saw the nationalisation of two banks, sharp increases in unemployment, out-of-control spending by government and a skyrocketing national debt, the country has been able to resurrect itself.

With an unparalleled track record in sustainability, the Swedish economy is outperforming all other Western economies on just about every front. The country once considered 'socialist' by its Western peers is now held up as a shining model of capitalism done right.

Sweden offers a great example of how a whole nation can come together with a shared purpose to preserve the environment for future generations. What can you learn from the Swedish experience to adopt in your own corner of the world and in your own business community?

The community

The word 'community' is derived from the Latin *communitas*, which means 'things held in common' and is a broad term for the feeling of fellowship that exists between people with a 'common' interest, purpose or goal.

Every business operates within a community. That community may be a geographic one or it may be a virtual one that connects like-minded people and organisations from across the globe. It's important to think of your broader community as a force field that surrounds all your other stakeholders. Your community has the ability to seriously influence the success (or otherwise) of your business, although it may not directly transact or deal with you.

> A business that gets on the wrong side of the local community can find itself seriously impacted. Indeed, a community has the power to dictate whether your business flies or fails.

Communities can be incredibly cohesive and powerful when they share common values, interests, beliefs and needs. A business that gets on the wrong side of the local community can find itself seriously impacted. Indeed, a community has the power to dictate whether your business flies or fails.

Tecoma, Victoria: mobilising a purpose-driven community

Since 2011, residents of Tecoma, a small Australian town in the lush foothills of the Dandenong Ranges 40 kilometres east of Melbourne, have proven the power of mobilising a purpose-driven community. For three years, locals have protested the opening of a McDonald's outlet in their town.

Despite claims that 9 out of 10 residents were against the development, the powerful McDonald's Corporation used its virtually unlimited financial resources to fight the council ruling in the Victorian Civil and Administrative Tribunal (VCAT), and some three years later the restaurant was finally opened.

The burger joint was built almost opposite a primary school and kindergarten and only a short distance from pristine forest, a beautiful natural environment that draws thousands of tourists every week. Residents are highly concerned about the impact on the outstanding natural beauty of the area.

Although the restaurant is open, the community is not giving up. They're continuing the struggle through the 'No McDonald's in the Dandenong Ranges' campaign and by spreading the word via their website (www.burgeroff.org), blogs and Facebook page. While the campaign was not successful in terms of preventing the fast food outlet from opening, residents are still fighting the good fight. What's most heartening is that they're now exporting the revolution to other communities who want to preserve their towns and who find themselves under attack from corporate bullies.

Of course McDonald's have their own side of the story to tell, but one would wonder why they couldn't find the grace and humility to walk a mile in the shoes of the residents of Tecoma and respect their wishes. Yet maybe this cloud has a silver lining. This monolithic, 'profit at all costs' corporate approach has been responsible for generating incredible community cohesion that's now starting to spread to other communities across the globe. Power to the people and to conscious citizens everywhere!

Here's a radical thought. What if this same community had campaigned *for* a restaurant they actually wanted while campaigning against McDonald's! Many of the conscious, purpose-driven restaurants now opening up all over the world might have been drawn to this stunning location and great revenue opportunity just as McDonald's was. Here's one such restaurant that I personally love.

Zambrero: empowering a social movement

When time is short and the fridge is bare, one of my favourite options is Zambrero, a quick-service franchise that sells healthy Mexican food through over 70 outlets around Australia. Their mission is to empower a social movement dedicated to the provision of food for those in need, through customer engagement and corporate social responsibility. Since Dr Sam Prince first opened their doors in 2005, Zambrero have provided millions of meals to those living in poverty around the world, through their Plate 4 Plate initiative. Every time I make a purchase, I feel so very good about my choice.

Communities have the power to divide and to unite. And they have the power to make or break your business. What are the communities that you impact? How do you engage with them? How do you work with them so everybody wins? How do they become your most powerful advocates so you never have to adopt push- and mass-marketing tactics ever again?

The supplier

Respect yourself if you would have others respect you.

Baltasar Gracian

I've never really come to terms with the way suppliers are treated in the marketplace my own company happens to be a part of. I regularly hear stories from my friends in business who also sell their professional services (as educators, speakers, trainers or consultants) about how often they're screwed on price and treated unscrupulously by larger companies that hold the purse strings.

A few months ago I received an email from a woman to whom I'd provided training services many years ago. I hadn't heard from her for at least five years. She'd moved on to another very large Australian company (one extremely adept at mass- and push-marketing). The email was very direct, showed little warmth and got right down to business. 'Our company is producing a series of educational videos for our small business market. We're looking for a small business marketing expert like yourself who'd be willing to present the series on marketing. We've prepared an outline of the content we want delivered and we have a price we're willing to pay our presenters. Would you be interested in tendering for this work and preparing a proposal for us?' And there were some other bits and pieces around what they wanted, but that's enough for you to get the picture.

My ego received a little boost at first, which lasted about five minutes, before I began to feel a little annoyed. I wondered why she'd sent such an impersonal email without asking, for example, if we might reconnect over a coffee for a chat about the project. And I wondered why she felt it appropriate for her company to leverage my reputation to impart a message that would not even be my own (let alone one I believed in) for a price they deemed I was worth, without discussion.

I took 10 minutes of quiet time to allow my irritation to subside and to consider the email in more detail before responding. I weighed up my options. Do I suggest we have a coffee or talk on the phone? Do I say I'm interested and respond to her request for a proposal? Do I say sorry, it's not a fit, but thanks for thinking of me? Or do I send an email outlining my new business direction and asking her to consider a new approach to marketing (the one being outlined in this book)? Finally I decided to send her a very nice, short and simple email thanking her for the invitation and explaining that her request was not a fit for the new direction of my business and wishing her every success with it. And her response? 'Okay thanks, good luck!' (Secretly I was curious to see if she'd want to know more, but no, that didn't happen.)

Opportunities like this truly are a gift. They're a chance to reaffirm our purpose, to remind ourselves of our values and principles around who we'll work with, what work we'll do and how we expect to be treated and remunerated. They're also opportunities to become clear and purposeful communicators and help us reflect on how we treat our own suppliers.

If we act like a dispensable supplier, then that's how we'll be treated. If, on the other hand, we adopt a partnership mindset based on deep mutual respect, then anything is possible. In this particular case, it was a lost opportunity for us both to become advocates for each other, even if we didn't end up working together.

A brilliant partnership with your suppliers can help you grow your business tenfold. Conversely, a poor supplier relationship can send you out of business. In reality, we're all in this together.

> If we act like a dispensable supplier, then that's how we'll be treated. If, on the other hand, we adopt a partnership mindset based on deep mutual respect, then anything is possible.

The alliances

An alliance is a pact, coalition or friendship made between two or more parties in order to advance common goals and to secure common interests. For many, the word is commonly associated with the political and corporate landscapes, and not always in a positive light. Alliances are generally made for mutual benefit, but not always for the benefit of all other stakeholders.

While Australia's major banks, media players and supermarkets would have us believe they're in competition, scratch the surface and you'll see that in reality they're highly aligned, or in alliance, with each other.

When countries align themselves politically with others in order to address terrorism, war, climate change and other global issues, again many other stakeholders suffer. When alliances are formed at a global, institutional or government level, it's so very often an attempt to control and dominate others—competitors, the environment and the public.

Conversely, alliances can be positively transformative for conscious companies where purpose and values are aligned and all stakeholders are loved and nurtured along the way.

For the purpose of this book, *alliance* encompasses the broad range of stakeholders that don't belong to any of the other most common stakeholder groups. Alliances can be highly strategic or can be small and informal.

Large-scale strategic alliances are partnerships in which companies work together to achieve mutually beneficial objectives. You may share resources, information, capabilities, customers, staff, investment in systems, information and so much more. Given the high failure rate of business partnerships and company acquisitions, strategic alliances are an extremely effective alternative in which all parties can benefit without high cost outlays.

On a smaller scale, alliances can take the form of membership of a networking group or industry association such as Business Network International, Business Chicks, Network Central, the Australian Institute of Management, the National Speakers Association, the Financial Planning Association of Australia or the Law Society.

An alliance might simply be an informal agreement with a complementary service provider such as an accountant, lawyer or stockbroker through which you cross-refer work to each other. This might generate a financial benefit for each of you (or not), and you may share office space (or not). Many health centres around the globe now bring together a range of health practitioners running their own businesses to offer a complete health service to the community. Then there's the ever-growing number of co-working spaces, where

> Partner with misaligned organisations or people and it can mean the death of your business. Partner with the right ones and you'll never have to adopt the 'spray and pray' approach to marketing and selling again.

business owners pay a membership fee to hot-desk, coming together at various times to collaborate on projects.

Generally alliance members don't trade with one another directly; they act as partners rather than work in a conventional supplier–client relationship. The most successful alliances I've seen are those where purpose and values are aligned and where each member brings their skills and talents to the table to deliver something bigger and better than can be delivered in isolation.

Who are the alliance partners you currently have in your business? What's their purpose? What are their values? Are you aligned? How can your relationship be stronger? What other alliances are needed for the growth of your business? How might you go about finding them?

This is definitely one stakeholder group that tends to form quite incidentally without much planning. Partner with misaligned organisations or people and it can mean the death of your business. Partner with the right ones and you'll never have to adopt the 'spray and pray' approach to marketing and selling again.

The customer

American businessman Michael LeBoeuf has said that 'a satisfied customer is the best business strategy of all'. It's not only the best business strategy but the best marketing you'll ever need, and the best way to stay ahead of the competition.

In chapter 6 I talked about the imperative of truly and deeply understanding exactly who your product serves and how your company serves them best. There's not much more to write here about the customer, except to introduce an exceptional example of a business that puts the customer at the heart of their enterprise.

bankmecu: the people's bank

While the big banks are clearly conflicted when it comes to customer versus shareholder demand, bankmecu, which is not listed on the stock exchange, exists to serve their customers, who are also their shareholders and owners. This Melbourne-based cooperative with an Australia-wide presence officially became Australia's first customer owned bank in 2011, but has existed since 1957.

Culminating out of a number of credit union mergers over the last few decades, the bank traces its history back to when credit unions were established by communities as a result of key industrial, religious and community groups deciding that the big banks weren't doing them any favours.

With a single share each, customers have an equal say in how the bank is run and how each will share in the benefits, whether through fairer fees, better interest rates, or improved products and services. At the same time they invest up to 4 per cent of after-tax profit in addressing a range of community and environmental issues important to customers.

bankmecu's success has come from embracing their roots, being committed to their purpose 'to provide responsible banking to Australians', their culture, a values-driven approach, service and differentiated products.

With products such as the goGreen® Home Loan, which offers lower rates and benefits for energy efficient homes, and the goGreen® Car Loan, which offers lower rates for safer and more energy efficient cars as well as offsetting the carbon emissions of the car for the life of the loan, the bank is leading the way in responsible banking products and services.

According to Steven Lynch, the National Community Development Manager, 'A large number of new customers come from word-of-mouth. This reduces our need to spend heavily on conventional advertising and marketing'.

'While we're mindful that great rates are important to customers,' says Steven, 'we're noticing a huge shift in the consciousness of customers and what they're looking for in a bank. They care about the rate and also about how responsible we are, what we stand for, what we invest in and our social impact.'

bankmecu is taking a decidedly provocative stance. 'We think of ourselves as challengers in this industry. We want to make it more responsible so that people get a better deal all round,' enthuses Steven.

This is how bankmecu came to be one of the 25 members of the Global Alliance for Banking on Values, the only Australian bank to be invited to do so.

bankmecu takes an inside-out, conscious approach to their whole business and marketing. They have a purpose and they engage their customers (shareholders) deeply with it so they spread the word. Eager to change your bank now? Try it and see what you can learn that's helpful for your company.

The employees (and volunteers)

Much has been written on the subject of why employees must come first, even before customers. I don't subscribe to any of it. In the new conscious business age, where everyone shares the common purpose to serve the greater good, why would any one stakeholder group need to come first? As I've said, we're all in this together. As a conscious leader, your goal is to create a culture where everyone shares the purpose and where you won't find yourself having to trade one group off against another.

I do, however, believe in the imperative of engaging employees first. They're the face of your company, the ones who can turn customers and other stakeholders on or off—for life. Employee engagement and loyalty are essential for the loyalty and engagement of every other group impacted by your business. If they are happy, they become your very best and brightest ambassadors.

> As a conscious leader, your goal is to create a culture where everyone shares the purpose and where you won't find yourself having to trade one group off against another.

A recent Brookings Institute report states that almost two-thirds (64 per cent) of Millennials (children born between the early 1980s and the early 2000s) said they would rather make $40 000 a year at a job they love than $100 000 a year at a job they think is boring. The report went on to state that Millennials overwhelmingly responded to companies that supported solutions to specific social issues with increased trust (91 per cent) and loyalty (89 per cent), and indicated a stronger likelihood to buy from them (89 per cent).

These findings are supported by Dan Pink in his fabulous book *Drive: The Surprising Truth About What Motivates Us*, where he puts forward the premise that people (including employees) are no longer motivated by the 'carrots and sticks' (rewards and punishment) approaches of the twentieth-century industrial age. Drawing on decades of scientific research on human motivation, he proposes that the secret to high performance and satisfaction (in all facets of life) is *intrinsic motivation*—the deeply human need to direct our own lives, to learn and create new things, and to do better by ourselves and the world... in other words, to be engaged in purpose.

One company that understands the imperative of loving their employees and engaging them in purpose is Etsy.

Etsy: reimagining commerce

Etsy is an online marketplace where people connect to buy and sell unique goods. You can find everything from handmade crafts to vintage homewares and unique jewellery on the Etsy store. Launched in Brooklyn in 2005, Etsy has a mission to reimagine commerce in ways that build a more fulfilling and liveable world. As a Certified B Corporation with 500 employees, 30 million buyers and sellers, and sales of more than $1.35 billion last year, they're seriously committed to creating an economy that is fair, sustainable and powered by people.

In 2013 their B Corp score was 80.2 so they rolled their sleeves up, increasing it to 105 points in just one year (an incredible feat for any B Corp). Etsy state their values clearly, beginning with the statement 'We are a mindful, transparent and humane business.' You can read the others on their website.

With a personal wellbeing score of 84 per cent, an employee engagement score of 84 per cent and an overall employee satisfaction ranking of 80 per cent (the average American company scores 60 per cent), Etsy really are dedicated to their people. They actively recruit and promote women in the company (46 per cent of employees are women). They are dog friendly and have a generous leave policy. They offer coaching and skills workshops on anything from herbalism to python programming, host an annual talent show and ski trip, and have a breathing room for meditation and yoga.

Etsy is a soulful company worth studying and engaging with on every front. What can you learn from Etsy and their dedication to their people?

If you happen to rely on volunteers (who are essentially unpaid employees) it's so very important to deeply understand them and love and nurture them just as you would employees. What are their roles and responsibilities? What is the 'value exchange' you are offering them? What's their intrinsic motivation for being involved in your organisation without financial reward? What do they need from you and your employees (transparency, feedback, ownership, integrity) to remain loyal and be your most passionate advocates? Organisations relying heavily on volunteers who are not engaged and rewarded appropriately are open to considerable risk.

If your company is not driven by purpose and contributing to a better world (or at least making an honest, transparent and bold shift towards it), you'll find it nigh on impossible to attract and retain the employees and volunteers you'll need for your business to prosper.

What steps can you take today to build stronger, deeper, more connected relationships with your employees? How can you make them part of your family?

The industry and competition

The legendary Buckminster Fuller once said, 'You never change things by fighting the existing reality. To change something, build a new model that makes the existing model obsolete'. And that's exactly what this new age of technology combined with consciousness is enabling.

Your competitors and the industry within which you operate are very important groups for inclusion in your stakeholder map. A good look under the hood of your industry and your competition might just be the single most valuable thing you can do to affirm or redefine your purpose, vision and values. If your business operates in a conventional industry that hasn't yet emerged out of the old industrial price- and profit-driven age, then it's vital!

What's the public perception of your industry? What is the media reporting about it? How are customers behaving? What are they saying? What don't customers like about the industry? What do they like? What rules and regulations are being challenged? How are competitors reacting and shifting their focus?

Rather than using the answers from this research in an attempt to become an industry colluder or to emulate the competition, smart companies use such research to build a totally new model that disrupts the status quo and transforms the industry landscape.

We're seeing it in the publishing, media, music and film-making industries. We're seeing it in the accommodation and travel industries and in the transport industries, with car-share companies such as GoGet and Flexicar providing short-term car rental by the hour. And we're seeing it in the grassroots economies where people give away everyday household items through websites such as TuShare.

SafetyCulture: putting workers and their families at the heart of their purpose

One company that's built an entirely new model to make existing models obsolete is SafetyCulture, a workplace safety company established by Luke Anear in 2004. In 2010, with more than 30000 businesses using their safety documents, Luke started their software adventure to build apps that would put safety into the hands of all workers in the world. Today iAuditor, is celebrating over 10 million inspections across the globe and is integrating wearable technology, an exciting new frontier in workplace safety.

Based in Townsville, Queensland, with more than 40 staff from all corners of the globe, their mission is simple: to save lives. They want to bring down the costs and make safety available to everyone so that workers can return home safely to their families.

> While many companies consider workplace safety to be simply a costly 'tick the box' compliance exercise, SafetyCulture has led the way by building a company that puts workers and their families at the heart of their purpose. This has meant they've not had to compete or play aggressive power games in their industry.

While your industry and your competition can be the very inspiration needed to build a new model, it's also well worth understanding how to work alongside your peers rather than fight them. It's imperative to consider your competitors and the industry as a whole in the delicate stakeholder ecosystem that surrounds your business.

When business is not doing so well, many companies rush to overhaul their marketing instead of taking the time to assess deep-seated public discord, industry sickness and aggressive competitor behaviour. They spend inordinate amounts of money on rebranding, clever taglines, sharp imagery and advertising, hoping it will 'fix' everything. They give their business a lick of paint when it really needs a complete reinvention.

But where do you start if you need to reinvent your business? You start by looking at your industry and the competition, and you make the existing model obsolete. And once you've done that, you embrace the competition and you take them on the journey with you. It truly is the way to mend capitalism and by doing so to make a positive impact on the world.

The shareholders

If it is not in the interest of the public it is not in the interest of business.

Joseph H. Defrees

Shareholders are vital in your stakeholder ecosystem, but they're no more vital than any other group. The Corporations Law legally commits company directors to maximise return on shareholder investment, but the best way to do this is to optimise value for all other stakeholder groups at the same time.

While there will occasionally be conflicts of interest between stakeholders, conscious leaders are adept at engaging everyone with the purpose and vision of the company, connecting groups across, up and down the organisation. They don't trade off one group against the other.

Management's responsibility to maximise long-term shareholder value very often means other stakeholders are sacrificed when profits are down and costs need to be cut, and the usual sacrificial lambs are employees.

Now a new type of corporations law, the Public Benefit Corporation, is set to revolutionise the corporate landscape.

Public benefit corporations are socially conscious for-profit corporations that operate in a responsible and sustainable way. They are managed for the benefit not only of stockholders, but also of all other stakeholders, including the community, society and the environment. This new legislation has been adopted in several countries and in 22 states across the US, one of the most recent being Delaware, the legal home of more than one million business entities, in 2013. Typically the legislation requires directors to balance the interests of stockholders with the best interests of any group materially affected by the corporation's conduct and the specific public benefits identified by the corporation.

> Management's responsibility to maximise long-term shareholder value very often means other stakeholders are sacrificed when profits are down and costs need to be cut, and the usual sacrificial lambs are employees.

The states' recognition of this new type of corporation whose objective is to create a positive impact on society and the environment is expected to have a significant effect on the development of this area of corporate law. B Lab (the non-profit organisation behind B Corporations), whose mission is to use the power of business to solve social and environmental problems, is the country's leading advocate of benefit corporation legislation.

This new type of corporation and the way it's redefining how a company operates just might provide the tipping point for millions of companies to move towards a higher purpose beyond profit.

> This new type of corporation and the way it's redefining how a company operates just might provide the tipping point for millions of companies to move towards a higher purpose beyond profit.

Whether or not the law changes here in Australia, there's still much that can be done to engage shareholders in the bigger purpose of your organisation and to help them understand that the pursuit of the highest possible short-term profit is most often not in the best interests of all stakeholder groups, including the shareholders.

Who are your shareholders? What would they say about this book? How might you engage them in a wider, deeper, more conscious conversation around your purpose and vision? How might they be encouraged to join you on the journey to becoming more personally and professionally conscious?

The ones you love (family and friends)

I'd briefly considered bringing family and friends in at the beginning of this chapter, but on reflection they fit best right here at the end. Because in the end, for many of us, our loved ones are at the heart of why we do what we do.

I do what I do to be a role model for Billy, to empower and equip him to pursue a life and vocation that is meaningful and purposeful. William Damon's profound book *The Path to Purpose: How Young People Find Their Calling in Life* reaffirmed for me the importance of pursuing my own purpose while setting an example for

> In the end, for many of us, our loved ones are at the heart of why we do what we do.

my son. The book identifies two crucial conditions for youth to succeed in life: they need to be in a forward movement towards a fulfilling purpose, and they need a structure of social support consistent with that movement. It's no different for us adults.

A friend recently shared with me that her father was a brilliant GP who dedicated his whole working life to being of service to his patients. He would visit them at home even in the middle of the night if needed. He was also a charitable man committed to many community groups. It truly saddened me when she said, 'He was never home. He dedicated his life to everyone else except Mum and us kids. I've had to undergo a lot of healing around that'.

Bronnie Ware, a palliative care nurse, interviewed hundreds of people in their last days, Her resulting book, *The Top Five Regrets of the Dying*, lists the five most common regrets they reported experiencing as follows:

1 I wish I'd had the courage to live a life true to myself, not the life others expected of me.

2 I wish I hadn't worked so hard.

3 I wish I'd had the courage to express my feelings.

4 I wish I'd stayed in touch with my friends.

5 I wish I'd let myself be happier.

Will these be your top five regrets when you die? Will they be the things that your family and friends regret about you too?

Engaging those you love with your purpose, helping them understand why you do what you do and what's happening in your life and business, will ensure that they're supportive when you have to put work first occasionally. Consistently sacrificing your personal and family life for your work is not the trait of a conscious leader, however. It is, to be blunt, an addiction called 'workaholism' and it needs to be treated like any other addiction.

Your loved ones can be the biggest fans of your business or they can be the biggest thorn in your side. You need them on your side, so spend as much (if not more) time engaging them in what's happening as you would your employees, customers and other stakeholders.

> Consistently sacrificing your personal and family life for your work is not the trait of a conscious leader.

I realise this part of the book has taken on a very personal slant. How could it not? After all, if you've given your loved ones the attention, love and compassion they need and deserve, you'll find it returned in spades. It's the very best security and encouragement you'll ever have to keep pursuing your purpose in business.

So who are your stakeholders and what can you do now?

Who are the stakeholders that need to be nurtured in your ecosystem? How can you ensure they belong to your tribe or business community? Of course I've not covered every stakeholder group to consider in your business. There are many more, such as the media, investors (if you have them), your bank and charities you support.

Now you know how to engage and nurture your partners, here's a simple task worth doing to help you identify who they are, what they need and how they might be uniquely connected to each other and to your business.

Use the tree in figure 7.1 to map out each of your stakeholders and then consider these questions:

- What do we need them to provide for our business?

- What do they need in return from us? (Not just money.)

- How do we ensure the relationship is equitable, transparent and sustainable?

- How will we communicate with them?

- How might they like to be engaged in our overall company purpose and vision?

- How might they like to be connected to other stakeholders in our tree?

Figure 7.1: your stakeholder tree

Of course there are many more questions to consider and answer. And of course you can speculate all you like about what your stakeholders want, but the very best thing you can do is actually to create a platform for ongoing dialogue with them, individually and collectively.

How about ditching the old-fashioned AGM and hosting a town hall? Get them all together in one big hall over food and drinks, share your purpose and vision, get real and tell them the tough stuff that's keeping you awake at night, ask for help, get them connected to each other, and share ideas on how you can all work for mutual benefit.

At the heart of a purpose-driven business is a profound understanding that what we all really want is human connection and to belong to a tribe. Your business has the power to build that tribe so that together you can do amazing things and make a difference.

Chapter 8
Promotion—how you spread the word

Without promotion something terrible happens . . . nothing!

P.T. Barnum

So let's now recap the Conscious Marketing Cycle, as represented in figure 3.1 on page 55.

We've identified that **Personal** consciousness, represented by the yogic figure in the centre, is the basis on which to define your **Purpose** (the why), and that your **Product** (the what) is the vehicle that helps you deliver on your purpose. We've also established that it will be your stakeholders, the **People** who share your purpose, who collectively advance your company.

Conscious leaders focus and refocus on these elements first, and by doing so remove the need for expensive traditional advertising and promotional activities. It is for this reason that the final element, **Promotion** (the how), lies outside the circle. It's like the icing on a cake, an essential ingredient that ensures it captures attention and makes it that much more delicious.

In this chapter we focus on the mindset required to promote a conscious business and offer some courageous and innovative new ideas to get your business noticed. I won't be going into a 'how to' of the various promotional tactics (that's not the purpose of this book and you can find that information elsewhere, including in my book *Marketing Your Small Business For Dummies*). These are the lessons I've learned over more than 20 years in the marketing game, working in my own business and with hundreds of other businesses. I'll also give you some great examples of companies that are already doing it really well.

Brand love takes time

> *Good things take time. Great things take a long time. And the best things take the longest time.*
>
> Author unknown

In the opening pages of this book, I put forward the idea that most companies undertake marketing for the short term in order to fulfil short-term profit needs. They spend inordinate amounts of money on advertising and promotional gimmicks to boost short-term sales with little thought for the long term.

Conscious companies—like yours, of course—are not driven by these same needs. You understand the imperative of taking a slow and patient approach to building brand awareness and getting the word out. You allow your promotional activities to take shape and evolve organically as you get to know your tribe and observe their response, and respond accordingly. You understand that the best things can take the longest time.

Here's a case to prove my point.

TED: 'ideas worth spreading'

TED is a sensational not-for-profit organisation dedicated to sharing and spreading revolutionary ideas through powerful short talks delivered in 18 minutes or less.

What many people don't know is that TED was born 30 years ago, in 1984, and was the brainchild of Richard Saul Wurman (now aged 80), an architect and graphic designer who has written and designed more than 80 books, including the Access series of travel books. He observed that the fields of technology, entertainment and design were converging and so launched the first TED conference event, showcasing the compact disc, an e-book and 3D graphics. The event lost money and it was another six years before Wurman and his partner, Harry Marks, made another attempt at hosting a TED event.

This time the world was ready to hear their ideas and the conference made money. It then became an annual event hosted in Monterey, California, attracting an avid following of intellectuals and visionaries from a wide range of disciplines in science, philosophy, business, music, religion and the environment.

In 2001, entrepreneur Chris Anderson struck a deal with Wurman to acquire TED. Through his non-profit organisation Sapling Foundation, Anderson became its curator and over the following five years launched TED global conferences and introduced the TED Prize. In June 2006 the first six TED talks were posted online, and within four months they had reached more than one million views. By 2009, the number of views had grown to 100 million, making some of the top speakers such as Jill Bolte Taylor and Sir Ken Robinson household names.

The range of TED products and services to evolve from the original idea of a single annual conference has expanded each year, the most well known of these being TEDx conferences in which around 265 independently organised events are held around the world.

In 2014 TED celebrated its 30th anniversary in Vancouver, Canada, with a live simulcast (TEDactive) in nearby Whistler. The theme was *The Next Chapter*—a consideration on the most important developments of the past 30 years and a glance at what is ahead.

Now with one billion video views, they've never waivered from their mission!

So what are the secret ingredients to the success of brand TED? Clearly it was an idea whose time had come. Yet it could so easily have died if Wurman and Marks had not shown the resilience and persistence to try again.

(continued)

TED: 'ideas worth spreading' (cont'd)

Today, because of this, TED is a globally recognised brand that adopts a conscious approach to marketing. They are driven by their higher purpose, they continually innovate to bring new service offerings to the marketplace, and they've built an outstandingly loyal following that includes everyone from event partners, to speakers, TEDx organisers, volunteers, employees and of course viewing audiences all over the world. Because of this, they've not had to use conventional mass marketing and advertising to spread the word.

There truly is no such thing as an overnight success. Getting started is easy. Gaining and increasing momentum for the long haul is the hard part. So many people give up early when they don't smell success from the very first minute they hit the launch button on their business. They lack resilience, persistence and the faith required to keep going and build a brand that people love. Don't let this be you!

Avoid bright shiny object (BSO) syndrome

When it comes to promotions, BSO syndrome is a very real distraction for small business owners and big business marketers alike. There are 101 ways to promote our business and it's hard to discern what might work so we get tempted to try them all. We see a program advertised on 'how to fill events' or 'how to master Facebook' or we're urged by a colleague to take up Pinterest. (Note the focus is most often on getting 'more' new clients and never about how we can better serve the ones we already have.) So we spend our hard-earned money and precious time attending courses or webinars to learn these techniques, only to shelve them when they get too hard, too labour-intensive or ineffective.

In writing this, I'm not suggesting that we shouldn't learn new things and try new promotional techniques. What I'm suggesting is that a helicopter view and a critical assessment of the value of different channels and how these channels work together are vital before we just dive in and do.

When Pinterest was first launched, I spent a whole day feverishly posting beautiful images of quotes and ideas relevant to business on my pinboards. When I awoke the next morning, I realised that while it was highly entertaining, I just didn't have the time to make it work for me. I was already committed to three other social media channels and I could barely keep up with them, let alone another one. That's one whole day that could have been spent mastering the channels on which I've already built a following!

There will always be BSOs in the promotional space to distract you. Take the slow and mindful approach before just signing up, and do your homework. Say no more often than yes to these things.

What promotional activities have you wasted valuable time on? What are the core five or six things that have worked for you in the past? Can they be used again (and again), and how might you make them more appealing, relevant, current and mindful?

Turn your attention inward

Our natural default when it comes to promoting our business is to look for clever and creative new messages and channels to get the word out to new audiences. This can take up valuable time and resources that could be better directed towards your existing and past customers. If you haven't truly taken the time to understand how you might better serve your customers and keep them coming back, then any effort in attracting new ones may very well be wasted. That's why it pays to turn your attention inward first.

Here are some sobering facts. The average unhappy customer is said to tell 8 to 16 people about their experience; 91 per cent of unhappy customers will never purchase from you again. It costs five times more to attract a new customer than to keep a current one. If you can make an effort to remedy your customers' complaints, 82 to 95 per cent of them will stay with you.

The old adage 'we teach what we most need to learn' definitely applies for me here. When I look back on my own business history, I can see many missed opportunities to serve my clients and workshop attendees better by understanding what they truly needed. I've learned a thing or two from these experiences and I'm definitely practising my own advice these days.

> If you haven't truly taken the time to understand how you might better serve your customers and keep them coming back, then any effort in attracting new ones may very well be wasted. That's why it pays to turn your attention inward first.

Whole Kids: living and breathing their purpose

One business that seems to be getting it right is Whole Kids, a company that produces organic food snacks (from popcorn to fruit bars and juice) for kids. Monica and James Meldrum founded the company 10 years ago when they couldn't find any healthy, tasty and convenient snacks for their kids. The Whole Kids purpose is to nurture healthy kids and a healthy world. They're committed to living and breathing their social and environmental purpose every day by offering products that are healthy (natural, wholesome, organic and environmentally sustainable) and by nourishing and nurturing the health and wellbeing of people and the planet. Also a Certified B Corporation, Whole Kids are a company dedicated to playing their part in the reformation of capitalism and the planet.

While clearly they're looking externally to secure major distribution opportunities, they direct just as much (if not more) attention inward—to the kids and parents that already love and buy their brand. This is evident through their blogs and website content. The content explains everything parents need to know about food additives, food allergies and how to discern the truth behind food labelling and packaging claims.

According to the Whole Kids website, childhood obesity is one of the most serious public health issues of the twenty-first century. Obesity costs Australia an estimated $56 billion a year. Australians spend more than $37 billion on takeaway food, making us the eleventh biggest fast-food spending nation on earth.

And this is what inspires the team at Whole Kids to continue the good work they do. They actively campaign for radical change to canteen menus, and they promote the importance of a healthy balance between onscreen and outdoor time through the Whole Kids Explorers club. They're also big campaigners against our junk food nation and for junk-free TV, junk-free fundraising, junk-free sports and junk-free checkouts. They're serious about engaging their followers and helping them take action on the beliefs they share on how to keep our kids healthy. They turn their attention inward to the communities, parents, kids and fellow supporters that share their purpose.

Whether you're launching a lean start-up or have an existing business that needs a conscious marketing makeover, these ideas are simple to adopt. Again, action precedes clarity every time.

Instead of always turning your attention outward to look for new customers, it really does pay to look inward and ask yourself some serious questions. Should we become a cause leader and an active campaigner to change what's broken in our industry? Should we focus our attention on building a better product that truly serves? Should we build a new product that serves the clients we already have? Should we focus on revolutionising our customer service experience first? Should we dedicate our attention to the relationships we already have in and around the company? Should we do something special for our most valuable clients and advocates?

50 per cent offline, 50 per cent online

I wholeheartedly agree with Peter Drucker's observation that 'More business decisions occur over lunch and dinner than at any other time, yet there is no MBA on the subject'. In the race for marketing mastery of the online world, it's easy to forget that marketing in the offline world is just as vital (if not more so). This message is particularly relevant for technology start-ups and businesses that have been built to serve their market primarily through online channels.

And by 'offline' I'm not referring to traditional radio, TV and print advertising (these will barely get a mention here). Offline is all about the *relationship-building* side of your marketing. It refers to the activities you take on that allow you to build rapport and establish deep human connections—activities such as attending networking events, hosting your own events, public speaking, coffee catch-ups, long lunches, roundtable dinners and one-on-one connections with others.

In Malcolm Gladwell's outstanding book *The Tipping Point*, he puts forward the argument that 'social epidemics' and large-scale change are triggered when trends and behaviours reach a tipping point and that the central roles people play in making this happen are as Connectors, Mavens and Salesmen. Mavens are information specialists, Salesmen are the persuaders, and Connectors are the people in a community who know large numbers of others and are in the habit of making introductions, as well as being good at tapping into resources, people, ideas and opportunities.

At the risk of sounding immodest, my biggest strength is my ability to connect people, and 'connectedness' is actually one of the five core values of my new company. In fact, Connect Marketing was the name of my old marketing company before I rebranded! (Incidentally, the other four values of my new company are courage, consciousness, collaboration and compassion.)

All of us know people who are connectors. Or perhaps you're a connector too?

ThoughtWorks: passionate about connection and education

Over 20 years ago in Chicago, Roy Singham founded the custom software company ThoughtWorks. His goal was to connect with, attract and employ the best knowledge workers in the world and to build a community based on attitude, aptitude and integrity. With more than 2500 passionate ThoughtWorkers working from 30 offices in 12 countries, from Australia to Uganda and China, ThoughtWorks is a conscious company with a soulful mission: to better humanity through software and to help drive the creation of a socially and economically just world.

Their three-pillar business vision is quite breathtaking: to run a sustainable business; to champion software excellence and revolutionise the IT industry; to advocate passionately for social and economic justice. The company culture appears to be equally breathtaking. Here's a snapshot.

> Wherever we are in the world, ThoughtWorkers share the same cultural characteristics and imperatives...We abhor and reject discrimination and inequality and promote diversity in all its forms. We proudly, passionately and actively strive to make both ThoughtWorks and our industry more reflective and inclusive of the society we serve.

So what's their promotional strategy (if you can even call it that)? ThoughtWorks people are passionate about connection and education so they've positioned the company around connection, knowledge and thought-leadership. In addition to writing tech books and blogging, ThoughtWorks host many face-to-face gatherings all over the world, from Agile Leadership workshops to Women Who Code meetups. They've really put some 'thought' into their promotional platform (pun intended).

I recommend most businesses adopt two to three online strategies and two to three offline strategies to grow the company. Each of these strategies should be well considered, complementary and driven by a seamless process to ensure they collectively make an impact.

There are three things to note here. First, offline marketing (stuff that promotes deep connection) is vital to promote your company (and even more important for technology companies). Second, education is a seriously good marketing platform for conscious businesses. Third, balance your promotional attention evenly between offline and online, every time.

> Adopt two to three online strategies and two to three offline strategies to grow your company. Each of these strategies should be well considered, complementary and driven by a seamless process to ensure they collectively make an impact.

Do less. Do it well. Do it again.

To be simple is to be great.

Ralph Waldo Emerson

In chapter 1, I wrote about 'the mass media minefield' and how we now have literally hundreds of channels open to us to promote our business, from bus-shelter decals to Twitter. I gave the example of poor Ken, the unconscious binge marketer who was looking for shiny new ways to promote himself without doing the internal work first. Ken is not alone.

The promotional landscape is confusing, cluttered, noisy and aggressive, and it's extremely challenging to get noticed in such a polluted environment. The problem is that most companies use too many channels in an attempt to make their mark, and they use most of them badly. That's when chronic marketing fatigue sets in.

> The problem is that most companies use too many channels in an attempt to make their mark, and they use most of them badly. That's when chronic marketing fatigue sets in.

In my former life as a consultant, one of the first tasks I'd usually undertake with clients was a marketing diagnosis and audit. Not only did I investigate fully the other P's outlined in this model, but I'd investigate their 'promotions' history over the previous few years.

In almost all cases, I'd find that people had tried just about every promotional activity in the marketing textbook, from networking to sponsorships, Google Adwords and LinkedIn. The word to take note of here is 'tried'. One woman, a financial planner, had attempted to run a series of investment seminars with her clients with the idea that each of them would bring a friend to share the experience. She believed it would be a great way to build more rapport with clients, share her financial knowledge and meet potential new clients. She'd abandoned this activity after only two attempts, to take up networking at other people's events instead. Why? Apparently just 4 people turned up to the first seminar and 10 to the following one. She had expected to have at least 20 — to 'make it worth her while', as she put it.

For any company offering a professional service, hosting relationship-building events (seminars, breakfasts, workshops) should be high on the list of promotional activities. While her rationale was sound, her creativity, ability to execute and commitment to serve (whether her audience numbered four or 100) let her down. But what let her down even more was her lack of persistence. Being good at anything takes practice and a willingness to do it again and again, each time a little better than the last.

She could have done a million things better each time to attract more interest, such as changing the venue, time, topic, speakers, format or even the invitations.

In reality, though, the reason many people seek marketing help is because

> Being good at anything takes practice and a willingness to do it again and again, each time a little better than the last.

a problem is occurring behind the scenes in the other P's of this model. This will always manifest itself in a need to do more and more promotional work, which most often doesn't work and is expensive and time-consuming. The lesson here? Do less. Do it well. Rinse and repeat.

Activate your tribe first

Seth Godin, the author of *Tribes* and TED speaker on 'The tribes we lead', argues strongly that the internet has put an end to mass marketing and revived a human social unit from the distant past—tribes. He asserts that tribes founded on shared ideas and values give ordinary people the power to lead and effect change.

This is the secret to building the new conscious businesses of today. Even if you do have the big bucks to spend on mainstream advertising, my advice is to activate your loyal followers first. The people in your tribe—from suppliers to staff, customers and volunteers (if you rely on them)—are walking billboards for your company. They have the power to attract or repel, not only new clients and new business, but major business opportunities, leads and connections.

Of course, if you've built a conscious, purpose-driven company using some of the techniques of the companies discussed in the previous chapter, it will be easier to activate your tribe to become your unofficial marketing department.

Wake Up Project: a world-changing, mindful company

Jono Fisher is the founder of the Wake Up Project, a company with the vision to awaken the best in people and organisations. I first met Jono in a café in Coogee, Sydney, around 2007. Even then he was a man with a vision to bring mindfulness to the world.

And now, some years later, he's well on the way to achieving it. Over five years Jono and hundreds of dedicated volunteers have built a thriving community of 50 000+ people who have attended 50+ sold-out events with more than 80 leading speakers and musicians from all over the world. The company hosts events with Google's Search Inside Yourself and Stanford University's Centre for Compassion, film screenings and the annual Mindful Leadership Global Forum, bringing to the stage such international luminaries as Brené Brown, Eckhart Tolle and Arianna Huffington.

(continued)

Wake Up Project: a world-changing, mindful company (cont'd)

The Wake Up Project has activated a tribe of loyal fans in one of the most ingenious ways ever—the Kindness Card, nominated by *The Financial Review* as one of the top 10 ideas right now. More than 200 000 cards have been sent out across the country. A Kindness Card pack can be ordered free online from the Wake Up website. The card asks you to do something kind for another person anonymously—a simple act such as buying a coffee for a homeless person or leaving flowers on a co-worker's desk.

I personally experienced the card firsthand some time ago. Lined up at the register at the best café in Melbourne, Kinfolk Café, I opened my wallet to buy a coffee and found it empty. A lovely woman stepped in to buy me one and handed me the card (not quite anonymous, but very kind). It was a humbling and serendipitous moment that got us chatting, which uncovered a mutual interest in Conscious Capitalism and led to an invitation to speak at her industry event. Without that card, this conversation would never have taken place. The impact of that simple moment remains with me today and I continue to practise random acts of kindness, with or without the card.

A conversation with Jono reveals that he's always had a bit of an allergy to marketing and indeed feels much the same way about it as I do. His small team of four staff definitely take a 'less is more' approach to it. Wake Up believe fundamentally in what they are doing and always ask themselves, 'Is what we are about to do really going to help people?' They've essentially built their online awareness through just three tools—a database, a regular email and a Facebook page. Jono's emails are brief yet highly personal. They're like receiving a warm, friendly (and often quite vulnerable) letter from him. And while they're delivered regularly, they're not sent like clockwork—only when they have something worth saying.

At Wake Up events, their approach is warm and simple. They have a well-trained, values-aligned volunteer team who greet people to ensure that every person feels welcomed and cared for. Meditation is practised at the beginning of every event to help people let go of mind chatter and stress. They pay particular attention to the aesthetics of the venue, activating all the senses and delighting all attendees with gifts on leaving.

The kindness that emanates from the soul of their leader, the shared purpose, the respectful way they promote the company and the deep connections made at their exceptional events really make Wake Up the perfect conscious marketing case study for this book.

While you don't need to have the soul or world-changing vision of Jono, you can still learn a thing or two from the Wake Up story. How can you activate your tribe to generate awareness, interest and commitment to your vision and business? Who are the people you most need to engage to do this?

Share your story

It's almost impossible to activate a tribe through the use of rational facts, figures, features and benefits. That's why storytelling is the new marketing. Stories open hearts, evoke emotion and build empathy. They advance us through the initial 'know, like, trust' phases in order to build authentic relationships in no time.

Stories can be shared with an audience of one or 1000. They can be shared through any medium, from blogging to public speaking to paintings, books and films. Stories are shared by leaders, artists, speakers, photographers, trainers and coaches. (My advice to any coach: limit advice and be liberal with story sharing.)

> Stories open hearts, evoke emotion and build empathy. They advance us through the initial 'know, like, trust' phases in order to build authentic relationships in no time.

Develop a list of finely crafted stories that you can draw on at any time. You can tell personal and business stories of your past that have shaped where you are today. You can share your *why I do what I do* story or your *imagine if ...* story. You can tell your story or other people's stories. They can be inspirational, cautionary or caring stories, or they can demonstrate your values in action. When telling a story don't focus so much on the answers to the *what*, *where*, *when* and *who* questions. Spend far more time on answering the questions that start with *why.*

I was thrilled to see Sandy McDonald speak at TEDx Melbourne recently to an audience of 890 TED enthusiasts. Her words were heart-warming indeed and were rewarded with a standing ovation.

What Sandy did so beautifully was weave together three highly moving stories—that of her father who lied about his age to become a bomber pilot in World War II at age 18; how the simple idea of 'knitting a square' backed by the power of the internet created a worldwide movement to provide thousands of blankets to South African orphans; and how the life of her first granddaughter, born severely premature, was saved.

Her theme? Stories save lives. From these stories, Sandy has built a successful business through which she helps other small business owners share their stories and create a powerful online community.

> Stories help you unearth and clarify your purpose. Power to the storytellers!

Recently Yamini Naidu (business storyteller), Jon Yeo (TEDx Melbourne curator), Sandy McDonald and I coached a group of 18 courageous change-makers to unearth, create and share their stories over a four-week period. Each of these wonderful people were given the opportunity to share their very short TED-like talk with a public audience of 120 people at a speaker graduation night, where their talks were professionally filmed.

The ideas, energy and enthusiasm generated by this committed group of visionaries were simply amazing. As coaches, it was such a privilege to help them shift from wondering and thinking about their purpose in business to speaking it and sharing it in the public domain. Stories help you unearth and clarify your purpose. Power to the storytellers!

In the business arena, there's no better investment for your marketing dollar than honing your story-sharing skills. Great ideas backed by a purposeful story and the ability to share it at will, whether on a TED stage or when pitching to an investor, have the capacity to power up your business and even change lives.

> Great ideas backed by a purposeful story and the ability to share it at will, whether on a TED stage or when pitching to an investor, have the capacity to power up your business and even change lives.

What stories do you feel compelled to share? How might you use them to activate your tribe? What are you going to do to get them out of your head and out into the world?

Adopt a cause-leadership position

One of my favourite American authors, Marianne Williamson, once said, 'Today's average American... is more apt to rebel against a tennis shoe not coming in the right color than against the slow erosion of our democratic freedoms'. Sadly I tend to agree. We live in a largely apathetic world.

However, the 'business as usual' world is being disrupted by a whole new breed of rebels and cause leaders. With a clear purpose and a deep desire to improve the planetary and human condition, these leaders don't shrink from their cause. They stand by their conviction and they won't change their position in order to win public affection. Cause leaders activate their tribes through sharing stories, outlining plans of action and making change happen. Cause leaders are people like Pope Francis, Marianne Williamson, Jono Fisher, Russell Brand, Senator Elizabeth Warren and Senator Bernie Sanders, John Mackey and so many more.

> Cause leadership is a far more active idea. It's about adopting a position on an issue that really matters, role-modelling that change and inviting people to share the journey.

Cause leadership goes way beyond the notion of thought-leadership. One could argue that the latter may, or may not, effect positive change and that it may, or may not, incite action. Cause leadership is a far more active idea. It's about adopting a position on an issue that really matters, role-modelling that change and inviting people to share the journey.

The B Team: putting people and planet alongside profit

Sir Richard Branson has always been a cause leader. He's disrupted many stale industries experiencing massive public distrust. He's pushed the limits of science with space travel and now, through the B Team, he's spearheading an initiative to keep the business world accountable for its impact on the planet.

The B Team is a not-for-profit initiative with a mission to catalyse a better way of doing business for the wellbeing of people and the planet. A global group including such cause leaders as Arianna Huffington (*Huffington Post*), Blake Mycoskie (TOMS Shoes) and Professor Muhammad Yunus (Grameen Bank) have come together to inspire other leaders to redefine the purpose of business so that it has a mission to create social, environmental and economic benefit for all.

Their mission is to develop a 'Plan B' that puts people and planet alongside profit, because clearly 'Plan A', in which companies are driven by the profit motive alone, is not working. Their ultimate aim is to persuade millions of business leaders to commit to a better way of doing business.

(continued)

The B Team: putting people and planet alongside profit (cont'd)

Critically, they've pledged to start at home by turning their own companies into world-class role models in order to gain the credibility so vital to engaging other leaders. By publicly declaring their intentions, these leaders are opening themselves up to serious peer and public scrutiny and accountability. At the same time, through taking a cause-leadership approach they've attracted worldwide public attention, the most loyal followers, and the conditions, opportunities and partnerships to take the B Team mission to a whole new level.

You don't need a massive cause like the B Team. In fact, most businesses have a far smaller cause than this, one that's quite specific and much more achievable. The surest way to keep the motivation high among your tribe, however, is to adopt a cause-leadership approach. What's your cause? What world problem (big or small) is your company dedicated to fixing? What action are you and your team taking daily towards that cause?

The giving culture

> *You have not lived today until you have done something for someone who can never repay you.*
>
> John Bunyan

We now live in a 'getting culture'. Everyone wants to get something from us (usually money) or to sell us something (whether we need it or not).

Conscious leaders do the opposite. They build a 'giving culture' in their organisation. They give their money, time, skills, products or services to people who need it most and who can't possibly pay it back. They give their staff what they need, when they need it most, whether it's time off, financial support or help through a difficult time. And they give their small business suppliers what they need, when they need it most, such as prompt invoice payment, regular work or business advice.

Conscious leaders have the capacity for *agape*, from the Greek meaning 'selfless love'. They do their gift giving mindfully, and never to the detriment of the sustainability of their business, because they know that their business is in itself a gift to many. And in so doing, the gift is passed on and the gift always comes back.

The JBJ Soul Kitchen: strangers become friends over dinner

The Jon Bon Jovi Soul Foundation is the organisation behind the JBJ Soul Kitchen, a community restaurant in Redbank, New Jersey, dedicated to feeding people from all walks of life.

Their vision: To serve healthy, delicious and, when possible, organic meals.

Soul Kitchen is not a soup kitchen for the homeless; it's a community kitchen where people come together to share a meal and make new friends. The food is healthy and nourishing and some of it is grown in their community garden. There is a menu with no prices and with choices for each course. The tables are set with linen, customers may be seated at random with fellow diners and everyone is waited on just as they would be at any other restaurant.

At the JBJ Soul Kitchen there are no haves and have-nots – everyone is equal. Everyone pays for their meal whether through volunteering to earn a dining certificate or by donation. Strangers become friends over dinner and they leave feeling that much better about the world.

Their manifesto is simply beautiful: 'all are welcome at our table . . . happy are the hands that feed . . . when there is love there is plenty . . . good company whets the appetite . . . friendship is our daily special . . . end the meal with a slice of happiness.'

Every business can learn a thing or two from the Soul Kitchen. Creating a giving culture in your business is not that hard, and it starts with you. It's the key to attracting the right people, the right circumstances, the right customers and the best of everything. Word-of-mouth spreads and before you know it conventional promotional tactics will be a thing of the past. What can you do right now to create a giving wave in your business?

Sell one, give one

For most companies a giving culture is created organically without too much structure or ceremony around it. It will be something embedded into everyday practices of the company as a way for people to show they care and are valued. It might take the form of providing chair massage to your employees, offering a share incentive scheme or giving customers a gift with every purchase. These things are not necessarily embedded into the business model of the company, however.

The 'sell one, give one' strategy takes the giving culture to the limit, as it's built into the very fabric of the business model. Zambrero does this with their Plate 4 Plate initiative (see p. 105), and TOMS Shoes does it too.

TOMS Shoes: uniting fashion with compassion

In 2006, while travelling in Argentina, American Blake Mycoskie witnessed the hardship faced by kids growing up without shoes. His solution to the problem was simple yet incredibly powerful: to establish a for-profit shoe company (not reliant on donations) that would provide one pair of shoes free to a child in need for every pair sold. Since then, TOMS has donated more than 35 million pairs of shoes to children in over 60 countries. They give different types of shoes based on terrain and season, and seek to create local jobs by producing shoes in countries where they give. TOMS shoes are given to children through humanitarian organisations who incorporate shoes into their community development programs.

Having identified other vital needs during his travels, Blake realised that the One for One® model could be applied to more than just shoes. He launched TOMS Eyewear in 2011 through which for every pair of glasses purchased, TOMS helps restore the sight of someone in need; 250000 people in more than 10 countries have now been helped. And in 2014, TOMS Roasting Company was founded with the mission to provide a week's worth of clean water in a developing community with the purchase of every bag of premium coffee.

When you take a look behind the company that is TOMS, you understand that their mission goes far deeper than this. They're dedicated to addressing the environmental and social impact of their products and operations and ensuring their supply chains operate under the required legal standards in each country. They're working on offering shoes made with sustainable and vegan materials such as natural hemp, organic cotton, and/or recycled polyester, and making shoe boxes with 80 per cent recycled post-consumer waste that are printed with soy ink. What TOMS has done so well is help create a movement that unites fashion with compassion.

The 'sell one, give one' model could very easily become a simple marketing gimmick, if adopted by unconscious companies looking for a way to leverage (or even repair) their reputation in the eyes of the public. As conscious consumers it pays for us to really understand what's going on under the hood of any company practising this approach, before we purchase. As a conscious business owner it might just be a strategy worth considering.

Whether you call the 'sell one, give one' strategy a marketing tactic, mindful gift-giving or simply good business, it is certainly a great attention grabber and a sure-fire way to build a movement around your business. What have you learned from this story? How could you build a 'sell one, give one' strategy into your business?

Produce content that matters

You may have heard the saying that in marketing 'content is king'. But what exactly is content marketing? Content marketing is the opposite of advertising, which aims to directly sell a product or service. Content marketing is all about enriching people's lives. It is the technique of creating and distributing valuable information that attracts attention and hopefully incites action. Content can be produced in many forms, such as news stories, podcasts, blogs, videos, newsletters, advice columns, articles, research papers, e-books, books, annual reports, media interviews, and via Google hangout sessions and webinars.

> Content marketing is all about enriching people's lives. It is the technique of creating and distributing valuable information that attracts attention and hopefully incites action.

What matters more than the medium is the quality and value of the message. Conscious businesses use content in a very powerful way to engage all their stakeholders in the company's cause. They showcase the real people behind the company. They produce fun videos that show their values in action. They write opinion pieces for the local paper. They write newsletters that are actually newsworthy. They produce cause-leadership papers filled with opinions and stories backed up with stats and facts. They don't advertise. They win hearts.

Winning a publishing deal with Wiley for this book was largely the result of my publishing the e-book *The Conscious Marketing Revolution*. One of my favourite pieces of content is *The Hero's Handbook* by Republic of Everyone, a creative agency dedicated to serving companies doing good. Check it out!

Hitnet: empowering marginalised Indigenous communities

One business that has really made great leaps forward in the content marketing stakes is Hitnet, a company run by two great women, Julie Gibson and Helen Travers. Hitnet's purpose is to co-create knowledge to transform lives. They do this by empowering marginalised Indigenous communities through co-creating and distributing culturally targeted information through a national network of touchscreen kiosks in some of Australia's remotest areas. Their content addresses chronic health and social issues such as smoking, STIs, teenage pregnancy, depression and suicide, in an engaging, culturally appropriate way.

Each year they produce an 'Impact Report'—not your usual dry and boring annual report, that's for sure! It's full of beautiful images and information on the social impact they're having as well as acknowledgement of all their clients, partners, suppliers and more. The report is produced in both print and an e-version and is distributed and read with great interest, not just locally but globally. It's like a brochure without being a brochure!

Good content makes people stop, think, feel and act differently towards your company. Brilliant content wins hearts and minds, and ultimately deals. What's your content strategy? What would you want to share with people? How can you get started on it?

Do some planning

I've lost track of the number of marketing plans I've written over the years. When the plans are first developed with clients they're excited and committed to seeing them through. In 80 per cent or more of cases, however, the plan ends up being shelved and going nowhere. While I'd provide the support for people to put the plan in place, most often the time and resources required to make it happen were just not available, or the client's circumstances would change, rendering the plan ineffective. It was one of the reasons I became disenchanted with marketing consulting. As an action-oriented woman, I really like to see people put into practice the work we do together, and in some way I felt responsible when this failed to happen.

> When the plans are first developed with clients they're excited and committed to seeing them through. In 80 per cent or more of cases, however, the plan ends up being shelved and going nowhere.

The technology age has revolutionised the way we plan and execute our company strategy. Conscious companies with a purpose and vision take a step-by-step approach up the staircase. They're active planners and are not wedded to lifeless plans that are not easily and quickly adaptable. Agile software development offers a method by which requirements and solutions evolve through collaboration between self-organising, cross-functional teams. These systems promote adaptive planning and evolutionary development, and the capacity for rapid and responsive change.

So when it comes to planning versus plans, I know which wins hands down. My advice here for small businesses is first to clearly articulate your short-term goals (say three to 12 months) and to get your basic marketing platform in hand—your brand and logo, clear messaging, a good website, a database, great content and perhaps a basic suite of promotional tools such as a postcard or brochure.

From here you can develop your marketing channel plan—that is, how you will get the word out to people outside your tribe. This could include up to six or more different promotional channels that are evenly spread between offline and online. For conscious companies with a cause, the most useful and essential promotional tools in your toolkit include sharing your great content through a digital channel strategy, public speaking, hosting events, public relations, hospitality, coffee meetings, dinners, referral programs and anything else that will help you engage your audience at a human level.

> Don't do marketing only when times are tough and you need more business. Do it constantly and regularly to promote your cause and you'll be sure to have a consistent flow of people joining up and sharing the love.

And that's enough of that. There are many resources you can tap into for the more functional and traditional considerations when promoting your business. Sorry, this book isn't where you will find that stuff. I much prefer you to be wildly creative and take a leaf out of the book of some of the cool companies featured in this book.

Whatever you do, make marketing a habit and embed these promotional activities into your daily business practices. Don't do marketing only when times are tough and you need more business. Do it constantly and regularly to promote your cause and you'll be sure to have a consistent flow of people joining up and sharing the love.

In 2010, while I was on sabbatical in Aix-en-Provence, I read a book called *The Artist's Way* by Julia Cameron. It is designed to help people recover their creativity and spirituality over a 12-week period. When I started the book, I found it extremely challenging. Readers were to complete one chapter per week and answer a myriad of what appeared to be childish questions. After the first few weeks of strong resistance, I settled into it and made the book and the questions an essential part of my day, alongside writing my memoir *Unstuck in Provence*. Without this book I would not have been able to develop the discipline to write 68 000 words in 100 days. Nor would I be writing this book for you now.

So whether you have a business book to write, a website to build or a series of events to host, make this work a habit, build it into your day and find the best people to help make it happen with you.

We know that traditional advertising and marketing no longer works. We simply have to find a new way. I hope this chapter has given you some great new ideas on how to engage your people and get the word out about

> We know that traditional advertising and marketing no longer works. We simply have to find a new way.

your company with a new approach to marketing. Your challenge is to think wildly differently about marketing and to make it cost-effective and impactful by building a movement around your cause. What marketing ideas have you taken from this chapter? Which ones will you toss around with your people? How will you get started on it?

The Conscious Marketing Cycle—it keeps on keeping on

Finally, let's review the cycle (see figure 8.1) so you can be sure you've made sense of it.

Figure 8.1: the Cycle of Conscious Marketing

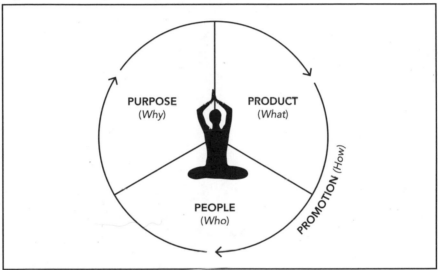

We've noted that **Personal** consciousness is the most essential ingredient of a conscious business and a conscious approach to marketing. Personal consciousness is the way to access and define the **Purpose** and vision of your business, and is essential to deliver a Product that truly serves the market. All stakeholders (the **People** who share your purpose) must be completely engaged in the purpose and interests of the company. Finally, once we have all these elements in place, we take a whole new approach to **Promotion** in order to build a loyal following and grow our business.

Conscious leaders focus and refocus on each of these elements. What grade out of 10 would you give your business for each of these P's (1 being poor, 10 being outstanding)? What grade would each of your stakeholders give your business? What's your weakest P? What's your best P? What steps will you take now to make some changes?

PART III
Shifting from theory
to action

Chapter 9
The conscious marketing shift— 10 solid principles to adopt

Humans are undergoing an evolutionary leap into consciousness. We're making the shift from ignorance to awareness to attention and action. We're no longer willing to accept 'business as usual' and we're voting with our heads, our hearts and our wallets.

Companies that ignore this change and maintain a 'profit at all cost' mindset will undergo a slow and torturous death—unless they're ready, willing and able to reinvent themselves. As I've shown, there's a whole new breed of conscious companies emerging ready to take their place.

The marketing function has an essential role to play in this shift. For many companies it can be the portal for the transformation of their business. By assessing customer and stakeholder behaviour towards your business and their response to your marketing activities, you can build up a picture of just how essential to their lives your company is.

So what do people think and feel about your business? How do they behave towards you? How do they react to your current marketing activities? What are people now reading about you, writing about you, tweeting about you and telling others about you?

Does their behaviour indicate an understanding and commitment towards you, your purpose, products and people? If not, what would you like their understanding to be? And what can you do to close the gap between their current behaviour and the behaviour you desire—without the use of manipulative, mass marketing techniques?

If you're committed to building a conscious business, this chapter will outline the fundamental marketing shifts you'll need to make to transform your activities from old-school unconscious marketing to new-school conscious marketing.

1. From profit-driven to purpose-driven

Profit-driven marketing and advertising campaigns dominate the marketing landscape. Their focus is on selling as much product to as many people in the shortest amount of time for as much money as possible. We see this everywhere. The Telstra *New Phone Feeling* campaign is one such campaign launched in 2014. The idea that having the latest phone will make me feel better and happier is simply unbearable to me. Give me that old phone feeling any day!

> [Purpose-driven marketing] shows you're a socially responsible, caring, ethical company dedicated to humanity and the planet before sales.

In purpose-driven marketing, on the other hand, all your marketing, advertising and communications are underpinned by a commitment to purpose. They show that you're a socially responsible, caring, ethical company dedicated to humanity and the planet before sales.

Patagonia: dedicated to implementing environmental solutions

Yvon Chouinard founded Patagonia in 1973, originally as a company that made small tools for climbers. Now with about 100 stores around the world, and with a full range of outdoor products and clothing for skiers, snowboarders, surfers and more, they have a mission that is inspiring: to build the best product, cause no unnecessary harm, use business to inspire and implement solutions to the environmental crisis.

Patagonia's commitment is to serve those people dedicated to the silent sports, the sports that don't require motors, don't attract big crowds, and that offer people the opportunity to connect profoundly with the natural world.

This love of nature also demands that the company and their loyal staff participate in the struggle to reverse the decline of the environmental health of the planet. The company donates time, services and at least 1 per cent of sales to hundreds of grassroots environmental groups. Patagonia is also a member of several environmental groups and is a Certified B Corporation.

They acknowledge that some of their business activities create pollution as a by-product, so they work steadily to reduce those harms, for example by using recycled polyester in clothes and only organic pesticide in their cotton. They're also dedicated to making products that last, and actively promote their repair service. And they're 100 per cent transparent about the footprint their products leave on the environment and how they're going about cleaning it up.

At the opening of the Black Friday sales in the US, Patagonia ran a controversial ad campaign starting with a full-page ad in *The New York Times*. The ad featured a photo of their bright-blue R2 coat with the headline 'Don't buy this jacket'. The copy in the ad goes on to say how the R2 and everything else Patagonia makes is bad for the environment. The ad closes with a call to people not to buy what they don't need, to think twice before buying anything, to imagine a world where we take only what nature can replace and to join their Common Threads Pledge initiative.

The ad received worldwide attention, drawing both the highest accolades and intense criticism. What the ad did was confront the issue of rampant consumerism. It made people think, it created conversation and it clearly demonstrated Patagonia's dedication to the environment and reducing their footprint.

What do you think of this ad? Would you have the courage to be so brutally transparent? How could you develop a marketing campaign that so clearly articulates your purpose and what you stand for?

2. From company-centric to customer-centric

We've all seen it before—company-centric marketing and advertising that's all about telling people how brilliant they are. You know, the ads that tell us how long the company has been around, how big they are, how many awards they've won and how they've outperformed the market and the competition. Yawn.

Customer-centric marketing impels us to turn our attention to what's most important to the customer. It taps into their own desires and needs, and it helps them to engage at an emotional level.

This type of advertising goes largely unnoticed and for many is a complete turn-off. This is mainly because it's very rational and functional and ignores the fact that most decisions are made for emotional reasons. What companies don't understand is that it's not about them—it's about *you*. Customer-centric marketing impels us to turn our attention to what's most important to the customer. It taps into their own desires and needs, and it helps them to engage at an emotional level.

Organic India: 'a chain of love, respect and connectedness'

Organic India was founded in the 1990s by a small group of people from around the world who had come together in India to meet the spiritual teacher known simply as Papaji. Inspired by his lifetime of service, this group of enterprising visionaries created a company that would help thousands of impoverished Indian farmers through providing training and education to cultivate sustainable organic farmlands. The movement took root and organic and biodynamic farming methods were developed and practised across India. The resulting organic teas and herbal products are now distributed all over the world.

As I write this, I'm sipping a Tulsi (Holy Basil) Licorice Spice tea. Take one look at Organic India's packaging and the messages they convey and you'll understand immediately their dedication to serving not only customers like me but also their suppliers, who are also in fact their customers.

Inside each box of tea is a cute little booklet that outlines Organic India's story, purpose, vision and values and that provides information on the Organic India Foundation, which is dedicated to providing health care and blood donation services, education for women, healthy infant care and hygiene, and blankets for those people without heating. It also showcases each of their products, from Tulsi Sleep tea to Coconut Oil, and their health benefits.

I love my Tulsi tea and I love everything Organic India stands for. They've won my heart because they care, not because they've outperformed the market or won awards. What have you learned from Organic India? How can you ensure every marketing message is customer-centric? What will you do to create such a powerful vision and message?

3. From price-driven to value-driven

I've already written about the price-war culture that exists in today's consumerist society. As our pay packets shrink (relative to inflation) and our hunger for more stuff increases, we're constantly seduced by the lowest price. As consumers we love it. As business owners we hate it. And therein lies the sad irony.

The price-driven culture is rampant. In the information marketing game, finely honed 'sell from the stage' skills are used to manipulate vulnerable people into buying expensive programs that are discounted (some by up to 90 per cent), but only if they buy today. In the fashion industry, end-of-financial-year sales have turned into end-of-season sales and even end-of-month sales. And in the professional services industries, we've already discussed the price-driven, 'charge by six-minute increments' culture of law firms and the like.

Purpose-driven companies such as those outlined in this book won't ever need to resort to price-driven tactics. They'll focus instead on what I call value-driven marketing, providing such value that price becomes irrelevant.

I'm not a great lover of grocery shopping (or cooking, sadly) and I've pretty much boycotted the major supermarket chains. These days I prefer to shop organic and non-toxic at small businesses in the markets that are a couple of hundred metres from my home. I love the idea that I'm supporting small local businesses while eating the best organic produce and using chemical-free cleaning and personal care products.

For the business owner, there are many marketing lessons to be learned from studying your local organic grocers. While they definitely charge a premium, they understand that their customers value their health and wellbeing above all else. And they practise value-driven marketing through offering the best products and advice and through having an extensive knowledge of the origins and health benefits of each ingredient in every product.

Many people shop at the big chains because of lower prices, despite the fact that most of their highly processed and even harmful products can barely be called food. I've had many people tell me it would be impossible to make ends meet by purchasing organic. But here's the point. Before industrialisation and the mass production of food, over 80 per cent of people's time and income was spent on producing, buying and preparing food. Today we spend less than 20 per cent of our time and income on food. We have simply reprioritised our spending on other consumables at the expense of our health.

As a consumer, what value do you place on your health? What other purchases could you abstain from in order to purchase real food? What legacy do you want to create for your family regarding their health? Being conscious of what we put in our mouths, on our bodies and in our homes is the ultimate demonstration of self-love and self-care.

As a business owner, getting caught in the price-war culture can be a tough gig to sustain. How can you shift from price-driven to value-driven marketing?

4. From masculine to feminine

Equal to the quest for consciousness in capitalism and business is the quest for balance between the masculine and the feminine. In *Unstuck in Provence*, I wrote a rousing opening piece highlighting the plight of women.

> I believe the most pervasive and systematic human rights abuse occurring right now in the world is female genocide and gender inequality.
>
> One in three women are subject to physical or sexual abuse in their lifetime. Every week in Australia, one woman is killed by her partner.

Women account for 70% of the world's population living in absolute poverty on less than $1 a day. One million women in the USA will be raped in the next 12 months. In Australia, women earn 82c for every $1 a man earns. Globally women earn half of what men earn. Only 4.5% of the Fortune 500 CEO positions are held by women. An estimated four million women and girls are bought and sold worldwide each year, either into marriage, prostitution or slavery.

Clearly, over the last 2000 years, men have created a patriarchal system designed to benefit men. This system is the cause of the current level of insanity we now find our world in. Sanity will only be restored through massive gender realignment and true equality, with the feminine traits of love, wisdom, compassion and humanity at the forefront of this revolution. The time for equality is now. But this is not a women's issue. It's a human issue—one that can only be resolved in an inclusive way by women and men.

Feminism has been given a bad rap because of its association with 'man hating'. The dictionary, however, defines feminism as the advocacy of women's rights on the grounds of political, social and economic equality to men. Feminism is the belief that men and women should have equal rights and opportunities. The 'He for She' UN campaign is a solidarity movement campaign encouraging men to advocate for women's rights. The inspiring opening campaign speech by Emma Watson, of Harry Potter fame, now has more than 1.2 million views on YouTube. Sadly, however, at last check only 186 000 men around the world have signed up to support the UN campaign on their official website. What needs to happen for this human issue to become mainstream?

> Sanity will only be restored through massive gender realignment and true equality, with the feminine traits of love, wisdom, compassion and humanity at the forefront of this revolution.

There are negative and positive traits associated with both the masculine and the feminine. The problem in the world of commerce is that we see an overabundance of the negative masculine traits, which by the way are to do with behaviour, not gender. These negative traits are control, aggression, power, greed, ego and competitiveness.

By now you might be wondering what this has to do with marketing. Everything. There is clearly an excess of the negative masculine traits represented in the world of marketing too. As I highlighted at the start of this book, the world is polluted with competitive, aggressive and manipulative advertising and marketing.

So what would the marketing landscape look like if these negative masculine traits were vanquished and the positive feminine traits of love, compassion, empathy, acceptance, gentleness and vulnerability were allowed to flourish? One can only imagine.

If your promotional activities put down the competition or are aggressive, price-driven or even sexist, you'd do well to take a look at the Cycle of Conscious Marketing again. This kind of marketing is really a symptom of other issues going on within the business. As you address these issues you can start to authentically address your promotional tactics and start to shift your marketing from the negative masculine to the positive feminine. Study some of the companies in this book that are doing it well, like Organic India, Soul Kitchen and TED.

5. From competitive to collaborative

Competition has been shown to be useful up to a certain point and no further, but cooperation, which is the thing we must strive for today, begins where competition leaves off.

Franklin D. Roosevelt

From the minute we enter school we're being taught to compete—for the teacher's attention, for better grades in class, for medals on the sports field. We've been brought up in a 'you or me' world instead of a 'we' world, and as we progress from the school system to university and into the business world, the competition becomes even more intense. We compete for jobs, for pay rises, for benefits and promotions. Ugh!

A toxic fear exists in most companies based on a pervasive belief that there's simply not enough to go around and that for our company to survive we must compete aggressively for attention, money and market share. Sadly, in the long run this kind of thinking can only lead to isolation and annihilation.

According to the ABS, there are an estimated 986 000 independent solo business owners in Australia. Incredibly, that's almost half of the registered businesses in the country. Many of these people have left the corporate life to start their own business, just as I did in 2001. They make their living from selling their skills, time and expertise. They work in thousands of professions, from consulting to financial planning to filmmaking, naturopathy, graphic design and art. They're highly skilled and experienced, well educated, well connected and talented. What they're often not that good at, however, is marketing themselves.

In the US it's estimated that by 2020, 40 per cent of the workforce will be independent business owners just like these people. One can only assume Australia is following suit. Interestingly, there appears to be very little information on this growing segment of Australian workers.

> There are thousands of people making the shift to wanting both purpose and prosperity.

I've taught literally thousands of these business owners in my workshops and seminars over the years. What I've found is that generally this segment of the workforce is isolated, underemployed and suffering financially. Over the past few years, I've noticed not only a growing concern around work security and financial stability but also a shift in personal consciousness and the uncomfortable realisation that their work lacks meaning. There are thousands of people making the shift to wanting both purpose and prosperity.

This market is fractious and highly competitive, and people are constantly screwed on price by bigger companies and pitted against their peers. Any corporate escapee new to this market, may find it tough. In the face of adversity, however, I believe there's great opportunity for solo business owners. If we could come together in a spirit of cooperation and collaboration rather than competition, we could become a most powerful resource for larger companies, who are looking for a more flexible, experienced group of talented and autonomous people to work collaboratively on projects.

Instead of all marketing ourselves to the handful of big corporations in Australia (only 1 per cent of the 2 million businesses registered in Australia employ more than 200 people), we could become the go-to resource for companies that are also making the shift to consciousness and that are looking for experienced, values-aligned people to work on their projects.

We could each make the shift from competitive to collaborative marketing, where everyone looks out for everyone else and where word-of-mouth marketing ensures business (and personal) success for all.

What do you think of collaborative marketing? Who could you partner with to make it happen? How would you change your marketing if you knew there was enough to go around?

6. From interruption to attraction

Interruption marketing is rife. It happens on YouTube through ads that you have to endure before every video you watch (until you can skip it), through door-to-door salesmen (yes they still exist) and through charity muggers at train stations (mostly backpackers with zero interest in the charity they are flogging).

Many find interruption marketing very annoying and it can surely damage a brand. I much prefer the idea of *attraction marketing*. Attraction marketing is really at the heart of the conscious marketing model. It's all about being a company with an offer that is so compelling, so different, so needed and so desired that people talk about you and actively seek out your business.

donkey wheel house: attraction marketing at its best

A great example of attraction marketing at work is the donkey wheel house building in Bourke Street, Melbourne, originally the headquarters of Melbourne Tramway and Omnibus company and built in 1981. In 2008, the donkey wheel Charitable Trust decided to invest in the premises and build a thriving community of socially aligned enterprises committed to addressing and solving some of society's biggest challenges.

Numerous events and workshops are hosted in the building, such as the Changemakers Festival and Trampoline Day. Tenants occupying the building include such enterprises as The Hub (the first co-working space in Melbourne), Kinfolk Café (a café that directs 100 per cent of its profits to four different charities around the world), The School of Life (the philosopher Alain de Botton's school was founded in London in 2008 and offers alternative learning to help people live a more fulfilled life), Streat (a social enterprise that provides homeless youth with the life skills, work experience and training they need to work in the hospitality industry) and The Difference Incubator (an organisation dedicated to growing investable enterprises).

For nearly three years I've been coming to work in this building and I can't imagine not continuing to do so. There's just something about the people, the community, the way everyone cares about each other, the combined commitment to serving the world and making a difference, that attracts me and the hundreds of other people who visit the building each day. I hold all my meetings in this building so I can open people's eyes to a new way of working and living. I run all our classes there and I attend many events there. I tell everyone about this building and the amazing people who inhabit it.

And many more advocates share my love of this building. (Even the Australian Prime Minister, Tony Abbott, visited the building in October 2013. While the response of the tenants was not so positive, at least we had the opportunity to show him what's really going on in the alternative business world that he might not otherwise have been aware of.)

DWH is an example of attraction marketing at its best. There's no need to practise interruption marketing or to use mass-marketing techniques to get people to turn up. What did you learn from this example? What can you do to become so attractive that you'll never again need to practise interruption marketing or mass promotion? When will you visit donkey wheel house and check out what I'm on about?

7. From complex to simple

Simplicity is the ultimate sophistication.

Leonardo da Vinci

Many companies today, particularly those in the energy, telecommunications, airline, banking and insurance industries, offer a complex array of products and services that can be bundled and unbundled, each with complex conditions, obligations and binding lock-in clauses. You really need to be a lawyer to fully understand what you're signing up to.

Complexity can also be found in the communications side of many businesses, for example in advertising, promotions, customer communications, websites and even billing. (All this complexity creates inertia making it hard to shift one's business to another company, resulting in *erroneous customer loyalty*.) It's a case of better the devil you know than the devil you don't.

Often you realise the full ramifications of this complexity only when something happens—your mobile phone is stolen, you want to switch energy companies or claim on your insurance. And that's also when it hits your hip pocket and makes your blood boil. But why do these services and communications need to be so complex and binding? Why can't they be simpler? Complexity is about keeping the consumer confused and shackled to the company, serving the company's financial interests.

Powershop: empowering the consumer

Powershop is a great example of simplicity at work. Backed by Meridian Energy, Australasia's largest 100 per cent renewable generator, Powershop is a modern power company that's designed from the ground up with the sole purpose of empowering the consumer and saving them money.

Meridian is a multi-billion-dollar company listed on the Australian and New Zealand stock exchanges. They own and operate seven wind farms and seven hydro stations across the two countries and currently serve 350 000 customers. Both companies are passionate about preserving the Renewable Energy Target (RET), which is to ensure that at least 20 per cent of Australia's energy is renewable by 2020. This is in stark contrast to the other three major power companies, which as I write this are actively campaigning against the RET in order to preserve Australia's reliance on fossil fuel power generation.

I switched to Powershop just a few months ago and have been delighted with the service, the care and the simplicity of it all. It took just two clicks to switch from my old company to Powershop. (I've had reps from each of the three major power companies knock on my door urging me to switch me back. Never!)

With Powershop you know exactly how much electricity you're using and what it's costing you every day. Their toolkit helps you control your power usage and regular discounts help save you money. Each week I receive an email showing me my weekly usage with tips and ideas on how to save energy and money, and each month there's a special offer to help reduce my bill. I can even store up energy credits to use in months when energy use is high. What I love about Powershop is the effectiveness of their communications, the simplicity of their contracts and the fact that I can actually speak to a real person.

Life is busy and we don't have the time to deal with the complexity of every day's homogenous products and services. The companies that rid themselves of complexity and make it easy for customers to make choices to buy, switch, leave and stay will be the ones to win hearts. Simplicity creates loyalty and advocacy and is essential in all things—from the design of products and services to your communications and promotions. How simple do you make it for your customers?

> The companies that rid themselves of complexity and make it easy for customers to make choices to buy, switch, leave and stay will be the ones to win hearts.

8. From unintelligent to intelligent

A few weeks ago, I accidentally turned on the radio in my car (normally I'll listen to my own music or simply enjoy the silence). Instead of turning it off, I decided to run a little experiment to see how many ads there were and what each of them was selling. What quickly became very apparent was not so much the number of ads or what was being sold, but how unintelligent and patronising the content and language was. When I returned home that night, I switched on the TV to view some ads. Same thing.

Overall, I was saddened by the quality of these ads. Apart from being loud and shouty, most of them were small-minded and condescending, talking down to us as though we had the IQ of a five-year-old and little rational, emotional or spiritual intelligence. This is true of so much of the advertising and marketing messages we're exposed to. Advertising (like much of the mainstream media) really does dumb us down.

Aesop: modelling intelligent, thoughtful marketing

One company that understands the need for intelligent marketing is Aesop, named after a slave and storyteller believed to have lived in ancient Greece between 620 and 560 BC and credited as the author of *Aesop's Fables*. Aesop was established in Melbourne in 1987 by Dennis Paphitis, a hairdresser and former philosophy student with a love of inspiring quotes (a man after my own heart).

His quest was to create a range of beautiful organic products for the skin, hair and body using both plant-based and laboratory-made ingredients of the highest quality. Aesop now has 43 stores worldwide. Every product is made with the same attention to detail that they believe should be applied to life at large, manifesting intellectual rigour, vision and a nod to the whimsical. Their products are presented in pharmaceutical-style brown glass bottles and jars, and each of their stores is uniquely different and stunningly creative. Their store consultants are dedicated to both their customers and the local community. The stores offer a full sensory experience, paying special attention to lighting, the scent of the store and the music they play, right down to the special touch of washing each customer's hands before testing products on them.

Words of wisdom from the likes of Carl Jung and Eleanor Roosevelt define the brand, which is beautiful, original and alluring. And their promotional activities are equally so. Their blog, *The Fabulist*, features articles and stories from prolific writers covering art, literature, architecture and beauty, and their multimedia ads are equally arresting — they're big supporter of the arts and literature.

Marketing in the beauty industry is generally very lowbrow and unintelligent, with hollow promises of eternal youth and beauty backed by celebrity endorsements and free samples. Aesop has taken a decidedly different approach — one that is intelligent, thoughtful and considered, and that has seen product sales increase year after year. How intelligent is your marketing and advertising? What can you learn from Aesop?

9. From duplicity to honesty

No legacy is so rich as honesty.

William Shakespeare

Much marketing and advertising bends the truth. It sucks us in and spits us out once we discover its duplicity. The diet industry is a case in point. Many of these companies have a lot to answer for. (Australia is among the top five fattest nations on earth, so clearly something isn't working!) In reality, it's simply not in their (financial) interests for you to lose weight and keep it off.

> Honest marketing is ethical, truthful, transparent and congruent. You promise a product, service or experience that you absolutely know you can deliver.

It pays to study the bigger picture in relation to many of these duplicitous industries. Do they really care about you and your health and wellbeing, or do they care more that you keep spending money with them? Taking a helicopter view of industries and their associated companies is always advisable before parting with your hard-earned cash.

Honest marketing is ethical, truthful, transparent and congruent. You promise a product, service or experience that you absolutely know you can deliver. (You don't promise permanent weight loss unless you know you can deliver it.)

Airbnb: connecting people from across the globe

As I write this, I have a lovely English lady, Claire, staying with me. She booked my spare room through Airbnb, a company founded in 2008 in San Francisco by Brian Chesky and Joe Gebbia. While both unemployed and in need of money, and with many of the hotels overbooked for a big industrial design conference, the pair decided to rent out some space in their apartment. They bought three airbeds and marketed the idea by creating a website called 'Air Bed and Breakfast'. And Airbnb was born!

Today Airbnb is a trusted community marketplace where people list, search for and book unique accommodations around the world, online or from a mobile phone. You can search over 800 000 property

(continued)

Airbnb: connecting people from across the globe (cont'd)

listings, from castles to studios and spare rooms, in more than 34 000 cities in 190 countries around the world. The company is now worth an estimated $1.5 billion.

Every property is associated with a host whose profile includes recommendations by other users, reviews by previous guests, and a response rating and private messaging system.

I've used Airbnb for business trips to San Francisco and winter retreats in rural Victoria, Australia. My experience has been outstanding every time. I love that I get to stay in a welcoming home with generous people in a real community, rather than in a soulless CBD hotel.

From a marketing perspective, it actually feels like conscious (and transparent) marketing is baked into the DNA of the company. In fact, as the community is self-regulating in terms of public ratings and commentaries, we're collectively doing the marketing for them! In many cities there are Airbnb meetup groups where people get together to share travel and hosting tips, and their experiences, with other passionate travellers. Airbnb goes way beyond providing a bed for the night. It gets people from across the globe connected. It exposes us to the true culture lying beneath the typical tourist façade. It opens up travel opportunities to those who don't have the financial means for expensive hotels.

And, in an Australian first, in 2014 the Victorian state government signed an agreement with Airbnb to provide extra short-term accommodation for people during bushfires, floods and emergencies at the homes of the 4000 or so people listed on Airbnb.

So many industries and businesses are duplicitous. Whether you're in one of these or you're one of its victims, it's worth taking a look at the business models and conscious marketing practices of companies like Airbnb. They truly do it right! What have you learned from this story?

10. From fear to love

Marianne Williamson said in *A Return to Love*, 'Love is what we were born with. Fear is what we learned here'. And we know that most marketing is predicated on fear—fear of missing out, fear of not being good enough, fear of your neighbour having more, fear of not being beautiful enough, thin enough, loved enough. So many advertising messages focus on triggering people's pain points in order to make them buy something that will fill a hole for a short while, even if it subsequently disappoints.

Eighty per cent of advertising and marketing has a negative overall impact on humanity. The shops in my neighbourhood on Chapel Street in Melbourne must strike fear into the hearts of any young (or not so young) fashionistas. I wonder who buys (and can fit into) the clothes on the anorexic mannequins in shopfront after shopfront?

It's time to unlearn fear and learn love. It's time to give marketing a love makeover!

Intrepid Travel: offering socially responsible, real-life travel experiences

In 1988, Geoff Manchester and Darrell Wade set off on an adventure into the wilds of Africa. Forgoing the comfort of an air-conditioned bus they had instead modified an ex-council truck and crammed it with friends and supplies and a case or two of beer. At some point during the trip, the two wondered if this type of small-group travel might be something others would be interested in too. Intrepid Travel was born just one year later.

Some 25+ years on and the company now hosts more than 100 000 travellers every year. With 1000 staff and more than 1000 adventure trips in 100 countries, Intrepid is dedicated to giving small groups (average size of 10) a socially responsible, real-life travel experience that is all about travelling, eating and sleeping the local way, using experienced local guides who take guests well off the beaten tourist track. There's no trip you can imagine that isn't available at Intrepid, from a Koh Samui sailing adventure to a three-day Uluru safari, from a Best of Turkey tour to an Antarctica exploration.

The company has worked hard to become a carbon neutral business and to keep money in the local economies they visit. The Intrepid Foundation is a not-for-profit fund that has distributed over $4 million to more than 75 non-government organisations that support health care, education, human rights, child welfare and animal rights.

The travel industry is a cluttered, overcrowded and aggressive market. The advertising atmosphere is polluted with travel options

(continued)

163

Intrepid Travel: offering socially responsible, real-life travel experiences (cont'd)

for consumers. So how has Intrepid managed to grow without competing aggressively in this market? They've focused on the inner circle of conscious marketing. For them it's about staying true to their purpose and vision and ensuring all their stakeholders are aligned with their values (integrity, responsibility, growth, innovation, fun and passion).

It's about taking action on their responsibility to the planet and to all living beings (they recently partnered with World Animal Protect to conduct research in South East Asia on animals in entertainment and as a result have withdrawn elephant riding from their trips—the first global tour operator to take a stance on the issue). It's about ensuring the customer experience far exceeds expectations. It's about building a loyal band of followers, from clients to employees to their local suppliers in each country. And it's about donating profits to causes that directly affect the communities they work in.

Oh, and they currently have a really gorgeous ad on their website that puts travel in a whole new perspective: 'Travel is more than the seeing of sights. It is a change, deep and permanent, in the ideas of living.'

As an Intrepid traveller myself, I can report my experience with them was one of the most memorable travel experiences I've ever had. If you're not much of a tourist, and you really prefer to get under the hood of the culture of another country, there's no one like Intrepid to help you do it.

As you can see, marketing really is an inside-out, 'love' job. It comes from within, from a deep sense of purpose, an acceptance that the role of your business is to make a positive impact on humanity and the planet. Positive marketing never uses fear to manipulate. It is authentic and real. It spreads love and joy and it leaves people feeling warm-hearted and affectionate towards your brand, even if they don't buy from you.

> Positive marketing never uses fear to manipulate. It is authentic and real.

Do you currently use fear-based tactics in your marketing? Does it work? If so, how and why? How could love work better? What powerfully positive, life-affirming messages would you like to share with your tribe? When will you give love the airtime it needs to eliminate fear? The opposite of fear is love. Time to make a change.

These fundamental principles are so very important when considering the many messages your company puts out into the world. How are you shifting your communications every day from fear to love, from complexity to simplicity and from being profit-driven to being purpose-driven?

Chapter 10
Your conscious marketing action plan

I wrote this book to raise awareness about the harmful state of most marketing today. It's an appeal for you to consider how you might reinvent your marketing in a new, conscious way. The Conscious Marketing Cycle and other concepts in this book are supported by stories of companies already applying this thinking (albeit unwittingly).

I'm hoping by now that you've scribbled notes all over the book, earmarked pages, shared ideas with your people, been inspired to learn more and perhaps started to take some action.

Just getting started on putting these ideas into practice can be daunting, so this chapter offers some specific ideas on how you can integrate conscious marketing principles into your business, and gives you a map you can follow.

Things you can do to take action now

Start a conscious marketing action group

Invite your business buddies to work with you on a regular basis, say monthly. Study the book and the resources listed in the next section. Ask a different person each week to present one of the ideas and stories in this book and to share with the group what they are doing in their own business. Invite everyone to discuss their ideas, the problems they face and action they need to take. Keep everyone accountable for taking action.

Engage your current networks

Perhaps you already belong to a networking group or you host your own events or conferences and feel like you've covered the old-school marketing topics to death? Why not introduce conscious marketing to your people and work with the content and case studies in this book? Invite me to speak or run a workshop for you in the flesh or via Google Hangout.

Find yourself a marketing buddy

Swimming against the tide of conformity can often be a lonesome journey. Know someone in your industry or a complementary industry dealing with the same issues? Why not get together regularly to brainstorm ideas, develop a plan and keep each other accountable?

Get yourself a mentor

There are no accredited conscious marketing mentors (yet); however, there are many conscious companies already practising it. Study the companies and the leaders you admire. Perhaps they (or someone in their company) would be willing to mentor you. Perhaps you already know people in companies who are doing this? Make a request for them to mentor you or contact us about it. If you don't ask, you don't get!

Create your own 'advisory board'

For many businesses a team of advisers can be very useful. I'm personally not an advocate of traditional and conservative boards as we currently experience them. I love boards that include people from every stakeholder group, from staff to customers to suppliers and professional advisers. If you love this book and want to practise its principles in your business, how can you engage your board in the conversation?

Be observant

Conscious and unconscious business and marketing practices are taking place all around us. Keep your eyes open and take notice of the good, the bad and the downright distressing. Observe what you love, what makes you feel good and what makes you feel bad. Your greatest inspiration will come from observation and intuition. Keep a journal handy and jot down ideas as you go about your day.

Hold a staff meeting

If you're working in a marketing division or are a business owner with a team of people, why not hold a team meeting to discuss the concepts introduced in this book. The book was written so you could share these stories. Pick the parts most relevant to your company, discuss them and see what ideas you can come up with. Meet regularly to keep people accountable.

Ask your customers

Ever wondered what your customers really think of your business and marketing approach? Before revamping the lot, take the time to ask your customers. What do they love? What don't they love? How could you improve the products, services and experience you offer? Do this research really, really well and you could find yourself with customers for life.

Do the B Impact Assessment

See where you are now and how far you have to go by using the B Impact Assessment tool. Assess how your company performs against dozens of examples of best practice on employee, community and environmental impact. This will give you a great gauge on the areas you can start to take action on and improve right now. Once you've done that, if you think you'd be right to become a Certified B Corporation, go for it. Many of the case studies in this book are Certified B Corps, so get inspired by them.

Join the Slow School community

If you're keen for a totally new way of learning with like-minded conscious businesspeople, then you might like what's happening at Slow School. Join our practical classes, short-courses, dinners and special events to experience conscious marketing in action. Slow School is the place for experiential learning, deep human connections and opportunities for collaboration.

Join the Conscious Capitalism movement

Conscious Capitalism chapters are springing up all over the world, from New York City to Arizona to Chile, Mexico, Brazil, New Zealand and Australia. Read the book *Conscious Capitalism*, join a chapter and get connected with other like-minded businesspeople on the same personal and professional journey. You are not alone!

Develop daily habits

Building a conscious business is not for the faint-hearted. It requires a commitment to your personal growth through the use of tools like meditation, journaling, yoga, other fitness and health activities, reading, time spent with nature and with family and friends, and joining like-minded communities. Develop a daily practice. (My daily morning ritual is lemon in hot water while journaling, a 30-minute walk or run, 15 minutes of yoga/stretching, 10 minutes of meditation and prayer. These tools have provided me with many answers to many questions. What are your daily habits?)

Start working on your manifesto and vision board

Who do you need to *be* to change what you *do* and have what you *want*? Your manifesto is a declaration of how you wish to behave, while a vision board is a declaration of what you want to have. Having what you want is not possible without a change in behaviour. Write your own manifesto. If you're not great at writing, say it straight first and find someone else to say it great for you. There are many tools and courses to help with vision boarding for business (and it might even be on the Slow School agenda!).

Join a co-working space

There are now more than 125 co-working spaces in Australia and thousands around the globe with members from both the corporate and small business worlds. I'd thoroughly recommend you consider spending some time in a co-working space. These places are hotbeds of creativity where ideas are generated and deep connections are made. I'm a member and avid fan of Hub Australia, which has co-working spaces in Sydney, Adelaide and Melbourne and partners in over 40 other cities across the world. And I've personally worked at Hubud, a co-working space in Ubud, Bali, and also The Hub in San Francisco. Most of these spaces offer the opportunity for you to trial the space as well as access great social and learning events.

Build conscious connections

Jim Rohn famously said that we are the average of the five people we spend the most time with. If you want a conscious business that practises conscious marketing, you may need to reassess the business (and personal) relationships currently dominating your life. Take a stock-take of those relationships or people that are not currently having a positive effect on you. Don't try to change them, just be aware. By changing yourself, either these people will change too or your relationship with them will change. At the same time, seek out relationships with others who inspire you and who are on the path you want to be on.

Become a dedicated learner

I've written a lot about learning in this book. The reality is, you won't change your behaviour or have what you want if you're not dedicated to learning. Formal tertiary qualifications are one thing; informal, self-directed, passionate and experiential learning is quite another (and is the future of learning). Avoid destructive learning that doesn't serve (for example, the mainstream media). Develop a positive learning plan for yourself. Go to a short-course, attend a dinner, watch a TED talk each day, read one business book a month, join a conscious business club.

Now you have some ideas to set you on your path, the Conscious Marketing Map (table 10.1, overleaf) presents a loose action plan that summarises all the things you need to consider while you reinvent your business and your marketing. Don't worry that some areas cut across each other.

Table 10.1: the Conscious Marketing Map

PERSONAL (YOU)	PURPOSE (WHY)	PRODUCT (WHAT)	PEOPLE (WHO)	PROMOTION (HOW)
Ongoing	Stage 1	Stage 2	Stage 3	Stage 4
What personal work do you need to do to make the business dream a reality? Who do you need to be, to change what you do and have what you want?	Why does your business exist? How do you make a difference? What is your purpose and vision? What do you stand for? What are the business objectives?	What products or services are you delivering to the world that fulfils this purpose? How do you make them so compelling that people simply want to buy and spread the word?	Who needs to be engaged and nurtured in the process of delivering your product to the world? How do you do it? What are the terms of engagement?	What marketing and promotions do you need to do to help spread the word and get people buying and talking about your product?
1 Changing habits	13 Purpose (what you love, what you are good at, what the world needs, what you can be paid for)	21 Products/services you offer	33 Community	46 Branding
2 Making time		22 Ideal clients	34 You	47 Positioning
3 Personal beliefs		23 Problems solved	35 Family and friends	48 Cause leadership
4 Dedicated learning		24 Customer outcomes	36 Employees	49 Stories and messages
5 Reframing success	14 Vision (how the world will look)	25 Pricing on value	37 Volunteers	50 Content marketing
6 Spiritual wellbeing		26 Doing your research	38 Shareholders	51 Marketing materials
7 Emotional wellbeing	15 Values (what you stand for)	27 Testing and refinement	39 Investors	52 Digital assets
8 Mental wellbeing	16 Start a movement	28 Product expansion	40 Suppliers	53 Promotional tactics (offline and online)
9 Financial wellbeing	17 Business objectives	29 Customer experience	41 Alliances	54 Social media
10 Manifesto	18 Financial objectives	30 Processes and systems	42 Customers (buyers)	55 Networks/contacts
11 Vision board	19 Planning and action	31 Resourcing— people, time, money	43 Customers (users)	56 Existing customers
12 Journaling, meditation, nature, exercise, prayer	20 Your business model	32 Planet and environment	44 Competitors	57 Sales and business development
			45 Industry	58 Database capture

Task: Option 1 (to be done individually or as a team)

An interesting way to use the map is to score yourself and your business on each of the listed items. This is a useful thing to do with your staff and other stakeholders, as their perception of how well your company is faring may well be very different from yours. It can become a great tool for discussion and help you identify the priority areas for attention moving forward. Grab a pen and write your answers next to each point.

1 How would you rate your current performance on each point (between 1 and 10, where 1 = *really poor* and 10 = *outstanding*, or NA—not applicable)?

2 Next ask yourself, 'What would I like my performance to be in the future (between 1 and 10, where 1 = *really poor* and 10 = *outstanding*, or NA—not applicable)? This will tell you how important each point is to you.

3 Next to this write the number 10 (the maximum score). So, for example, it might look like this: '1. Changing habits 3/8/10'.

4 Total each of the scores and compare against the maximum possible score of 580. Calculate your current and future desired performance as a percentage of 580.

5 Next, measure the gap between your performance and the performance you seek for each point. If the gap is 5 or more it suggests this area is a priority for you. If, for example, you've given point *25: Pricing on value* a score of just 1 but would like it to be an 8, then this becomes a priority.

6 On a separate sheet of paper write down why there's such a gap and come up with three things you can do now to start to reduce it. Less is more here. No doubt you and your team will have 20 different ideas on how you can improve things, but really you only need one to get started. Taking a small step in the right direction is better than having hundreds of clever ideas never executed. Remember, action precedes clarity.

Task: Option 2 (to be done with your team)

Another great way to use the Conscious Marketing Map is to play the 'What's working? What's not working?' game. After your people have read the book, gather them together and hand them the map and a pad of small sticky notes. Ask them to take 10 minutes to write down all the things that are working in the business (this may include things not listed on the map). Then ask them to spend 10 minutes writing down all the things that are *not* working in the business. Ensure there's only one point on each sticky note.

Once you've gathered everyone's sticky notes, categorise them according to one of the 5 P's and identify the most urgent issues that need to be addressed. You can then work out a plan of action on how to address these things.

No doubt you or your team will have some other ideas that you can use to facilitate discussion and action. If you don't have the facilitation skills or think it might be better facilitated by a third party, look for a qualified person (or contact me to see what I might suggest).

This chapter has offered you some useful tools to help you integrate conscious marketing into your business. If you feel you have a long way to go, don't be deterred. We all do, including the companies showcased in this book. No one is perfect. Indeed, who wants to be perfect anyway? Take one action each day and see just how far you will have come in a week, a month, a year and a decade from now. One thing is certain: business as usual and doing nothing new are not options!

CONCLUSION

I began this book with a very loud and open declaration that marketing is broken. If you're still with me here, I assume you must agree. We simply can't fix anything until we acknowledge it's broken. And we can't fix anything with the same thinking that caused the problem in the first place. That's why we journeyed through the realms of consciousness to uncover ideas on how we can become more conscious both as human beings and as business leaders.

I then applied consciousness to marketing and presented an alternative marketing model for you to consider — the Cycle of Conscious Marketing, with its five core P's (Personal, Purpose, Product, People and Promotion). We discussed 10 big things to consider in shifting our promotional efforts from an unconscious to a conscious level. And we finished by considering the Conscious Marketing Map and some practical ideas on how to implement the ideas in this book.

The companies whose stories are introduced in the case studies exemplify conscious and mindful business practice. They purposefully and passionately serve the best interests of humanity and the planet. Of course I don't know everything going on under the hood of each of these companies, but I am convinced they represent the best that the world of capitalism has to offer right now.

My sincere wish is that within the next two decades conscious business and marketing practices will be the norm, and not the exception as they are today, and that reading a book like this will therefore be rendered unnecessary.

My wish is for us all to take a bee-like approach to creating and marketing an awesome business. For bees to survive and thrive they rely on fellow bees, a beehive to come home to and a healthy, delicately balanced ecosystem. The world of business and capitalism is no different. It's in our interests to serve the whole of humanity and the planet, not just our own.

Capitalism is sick, and the business world has much to answer for. We've blindly robbed our children of their future, and we each have a role to play in turning it around. What will you contribute? How will your business help solve the world's most intractable problems? What will you do today, tomorrow, next week, next month, next year? Write to me and tell me about it. I promise to respond.

AFTERWORD BY BILLY STAFFORD

I'm a 17-year-old student just finishing Year 11 and I'm about to approach the holiday season before undergoing my final year at high school.

While I'm very thankful for the school that I go to, I can't wait to start life on my own terms. The past 12 years have been great, but after a while you get tired of school bells, uniforms and the same people every day.

While my mum wrote this book about business and capitalism and marketing, I know that she wrote it for my generation and me. She's passionate about so many things like ensuring businesses do good, gender equality, changing the education system and improving our environment.

Mum can be painful to be around when she gets started, but mostly I admire her and really respect that she stands up for what she believes in without caring what other people think.

I think one thing my mother and my generation have in common is that we share similar values. I know that my generation will be responsible for creating a more equal society, better governments and a healthier environment.

I believe the education system should change so that this can happen—and many of my teachers actually believe this too. I wish every kid could have an education that is right for them, one that helps them find their passion and purpose, do work they love and that makes a difference to others. I'm lucky that my Mum and Dad want me to do what I love. They want me to chase a dream, not a pay cheque.

Us youth get asked the same question so often…what do you want to be? Truth is, I don't know what I want to be. I only know what I love to do. I love writing, spending time with mates and family, politics, history, laughing, singing and above all—helping people. Helping people is really what I get the most enjoyment out of. It makes me happy to make others happy, which is why you'll always find me involved in some kind of community service work at school.

All I know is that I want to help people when I leave school. After university, I want to help people on a large scale, globally, by working in a conscious business.

I hope that you've enjoyed mum's book and that it will inspire you to do something big to make your business a better one for people and the planet. One good business can change thousands of lives. Make it count.

THE
CONSCIOUS
MARKETING
MANIFESTO

The Conscious Marketing Manifesto on the following pages is a summary of all this book covers. It's a public declaration of how marketing can change and become a force for good both in your company and in the world. Review it regularly as you go about your business and market your services to the public.

conscious marketing

Build something so fundamentally good and compelling right into the heart of your business, products and services that people simply want to join your business community (tribe) to spread the word.

Commit to the five P's
Personal. Purpose. Product. People. Promotion.

It's your life. It's **personal**.
Do the inner work. Dig deep.
Ask brilliant questions. Question every answer.
Unlearn the old. Study the new.
Be both a teacher and a student.
Dig even deeper. Journal. Meditate.
Pray. Connect with like-minded souls.
Get comfortable with being uncomfortable.
Take action, knowing it precedes clarity.
Write your own manifesto. Create your vision board.
Read a lot. Watch TED talks.
You'll find your why.

Just as bees build hives, conscious beings build conscious companies.

It's your vocation. It's personal.
Study what's broken and pledge to fix it.
Do something good. Advance humanity.
Slow down. Regenerate our planet.
It's for our kids and their kids too.
Declare your business **purpose**.
It's your glue. Don't compromise.
Build the best **products**.
Engage your **people** in the process.
Let your customers be the judge.
Be ready, willing and able to adapt.
Ask. Listen. Serve. Care. Give.
Generate great loyalty. Become a cause leader.
Create a movement. Activate your tribe.
Do outstanding things for them.
Remember always, who cares
matters and who matters cares.
Promote wisely. Get creative. Do less.
Do it well. Do it again.
Use real stories. Less head. More heart.
Joy. Hope. Love. No trade-offs.

Make the shift:

From profit-driven to purpose-driven.

From company-centric to customer-centric.

From price-driven to value-driven.

From competitive to collaborative.

From interruption to attraction.

From duplicity to honesty.

From complexity to simplicity.

From masculine to feminine.

From unintelligent to intelligent

From fear to love.

This is your life. This is your livelihood.
It's time to make a change.

USEFUL RESOURCES FOR CONSCIOUS BUSINESS OWNERS

Company websites (W), books (B), videos/movies/TED talks (V)

A New Earth (B), Eckhart Tolle,

Aesop (W), www.aesop.com www.eckharttolle.com

Airbnb (W), www.airbnb.com.au

The Artist's Way (B), Julia Cameron, juliacameronlive.com

Atlassian (W), www.atlassian.com

Australian Ethical (W), www.australianethical.com.au

B Corporation (W), www.bcorporation.net

B Impact Assessment (W), www.bimpactassessment.net

B Team (W), www.bteam.org

bankmecu (W), www.bankmecu.com.au

Benefit Capital (W), www.benefit.capital

Benefit Corporation (W), www.benefitcorp.net

Bitcoin (W), www.bitcoin.org

Breaking the Time Barrier (B), Freshbooks, breakingthetimebarrier
.freshbooks.com

Business Model Generation (B), Alexander Osterwalder and Yves Pigneur

Clearpoint Counsel (W), www.clearpointcounsel.com

The Co-Learners (W), thecolearners.net

Conscious Capitalism (B), John Mackey and Rajendra Sisodia

Conscious Capitalism Australia (W), www.consciouscapitalism.org.au

Conscious Capitalism (W; global)W, www.consciouscapitalism.org

The Corporation (V), thecorporation.com

Creating Brand Energy (B), Cath Sutherland, www.consciousbusiness.net.au

The Customer Service Training Group (W), www
.customerservicetraininggroup.com.au

The Difference Incubator (W), tdi.org.au

donkey wheel house (W), donkeywheelhouse.org

Drive (B), Dan Pink, www.danpink.com/books/drive

Dumbo Feather (B), www.dumbofeather.com/

Ecocreative (W), www.ecocreative.com.au

The Ecology of Commerce (B), Paul Hawken, www.paulhawken.com

Ecostore (W), www.ecostore.com.au

Etsy (W), www.etsy.com

Firms of Endearment (B), Raj Sisodia, firmsofendearment.com

Global Banking Alliance on Values (W), www.gabv.org

Hitnet (W), www.hitnet.com.au

Holacracy (W), holacracy.org

Holstee Manifesto (W), www.holstee.com/pages/about

How Great Leaders Inspire Action (V), Simon Sinek, www.ted.com

How Schools Kill Creativity (V), Ken Robinson, www.ted.com

Hub Australia (W), hubaustralia.com

The Hunger Project (W), www.thp.org.au

Impact Investment Group (W), www.impact-group.com.au

In Praise of Slow (B), Carl Honoré

Interface Inc. (W), www.interface.com

The Inside Job (V), www.imdb.com/title/tt1645089

Intrepid Travel (W), www.intrepidtravel.com

It's Not What You Sell; It's What You Stand For (B), Roy Spence, www.itsnotwhatyousell.com

KeepCup (W), www.keepcup.com.au

Kickstarter (W), www.kickstarter.com

Kinfolk Café (W), www.kinfolk.org.au

Liberating the Corporate Soul (B), Richard Barrett

Man's Search for Meaning (B), Victor Frankl

Marque Lawyers (W), www.marquelawyers.com.au

Nudge Accounting (W), www.nudgeaccounting.com.au

On the Business Logic of Sustainability (V), Ray Anderson, www.ted.com

Oursay (W), www.oursay.org

Organic India (W), www.organicindia.com

Outliers (B), Malcolm Gladwell, www.gladwell.com/outliers

Patagonia (W), www.patagonia.com/international

Path to Purpose (B), William Damon, www.williamdamon.com/pathtopurpose.html

The Power of Now (B), Eckhart Tolle, www.eckharttolle.com

The Power of Vulnerability (V), Brené Brown, www.ted.com

Powershop (W), www.powershop.com.au

Pozible (W), www.pozible.com

Sacred Economics (W), sacred-economics.com

Safety Culture (W), www.safetyculture.com.au

The School of Life (W), www.theschooloflife.com

The Slow School of Business (W), www.slowschool.com.au

Small Giants (W), www.smallgiants.com.au

The Soul Kitchen (W), www.jbjsoulkitchen.org

Soul of Money (W), www.lynnetwist.com

Southwest Airlines (W), www.southwest.com

Spiritual Capital (B), Danah Zohar

The Story of Stuff (W), storyofstuff.org

TED (W), www.ted.com

TEDx Melbourne (W), tedxmelbourne.com

ThoughtWorks (W), www.thoughtworks.com

The Tipping Point (B), Malcolm Gladwell, www.gladwell.com/the-tipping-point

TOMS Shoes (W), www.toms.com

The Top Five Regrets of the Dying (B), Bronnie Ware

Tribes (B), Seth Godin, www.sethgodin.com

TuShare (W), www.tushare.com

Wake Up Project and Kindness Cards (W), wakeupproject.com.au

Whole Foods Market (W), www.wholefoodsmarket.com

Whole Kids (W), www.wholekids.com.au

Zambrero (W), www.patagonia.com/international

Zappos (W), www.zappos.com

INDEX

Connect
with WILEY ▶▶▶

WILEY

Browse and purchase the full range of Wiley publications on our official website.

www.wiley.com

Check out the Wiley blog for news, articles and information from Wiley and our authors.

www.wileybizaus.com

Join the conversation on Twitter and keep up to date on the latest news and events in business.

@WileyBizAus

Sign up for Wiley newsletters to learn about our latest publications, upcoming events and conferences, and discounts available to our customers.

www.wiley.com/email

Wiley titles are also produced in e-book formats. Available from all good retailers.

WILEY

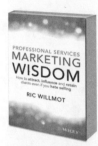

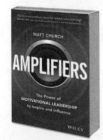